Battleground series:

With the continued expansion of the Battleground Series a **Battleground Series Club** has been formed to benefit the reader. The purpose of the Club is to keep members informed of new titles and to offer many other reader-benefits. Membership is free and by registering an interest you can help us predict print runs and thus assist us in maintaining the quality and prices at their present levels.
Please call the office on 01226 734555, or send your name and address along with a request for more information to:

Battleground Series Club Pen & Sword Books Ltd,
47 Church Street, Barnsley, South Yorkshire S70 2AS

IN PURSUIT OF HITLER

IN PURSUIT OF HITLER

Battles through the Nazi heartland March to May 1945

ANDREW RAWSON

Pen & Sword
MILITARY

First published in Great Britain in 2008 by
Pen & Sword Military
an imprint of
Pen & Sword Books Ltd
47 Church Street
Barnsley
South Yorkshire
S70 2AS

Copyright © Andrew Rawson, 2008

ISBN 978 1844 155613

Printed and bound in the United Kingdom by CPI

Pen & Sword Books Ltd incorporates the imprints of Pen & Sword Aviation, Pen & Sword
Maritime, Pen & Sword Military, Wharncliffe Local History, Pen and Sword Select,
Pen and Sword Military Classics and Leo Cooper.

For a complete list of Pen & Sword titles, please contact
Pen & Sword Books Limited
47 Church Street, Barnsley, South Yorkshire, S70 2AS, England
E-mail: enquiries@pen-and-sword.co.uk
Website: www.pen-and-sword.co.uk

CONTENTS

ACKNOWLEDGEMENTS

Many people at various museums in England, America and Germany have helped me during the preparation of this book and a few deserve a special mention. Randall Lewis obtained copies of many obscure American unit histories from the Library of Congress in Washington DC. Holly Reid in the photograph archive at the American National Archives, also in Washington DC, guided me through the enormous collection of images. Peter Dome was extremely helpful with the chapter on the Hammelburg Raid and his website, www.taskforcebaum.com, is well worth visiting if you want to find out more about the raid.

Finally, I have to thank Roni Wilkinson at Pen and Sword, not only for putting the book together, but also for suggesting the original idea to cover Bavaria for the Battleground Series. Little did he know I would take him up on the challenge and ride my motorcycle from the Rhine to the Eagle's Nest. He so looks forward to my 'guess where I am now?' phone calls.

I dedicate this book to my son Alex who at fourteen has already been to several battlefields across Europe and will no doubt visit many more. Let us hope that his generation draw the correct conclusions from books such as these.

After a year in Landsberg prison Hitler left in December 1924 and began to reform the National Socialist Party.

INTRODUCTION

This book traces a route across southern Germany, starting at the Rhine, south of Frankfurt-am-Main, and winds its way through Wurzburg, Nuremberg, Munich to Berchtesgaden in the Alps. Two stories intertwine along the way. The first is the rise and fall of the Nazis while the second covers the American advance across the region in March and April 1945. The narrative describes events in the order that they are found along the route, however, most chapters can be read as a separate story if you wish. Travel directions are given in the narrative. Again the visitor can follow the entire route or choose to visit one or more sites and follow their own routes. The two timelines put many of the locations and events covered in the book into chronological order.

The Nazis' Rise to Power

1919

September	Adolf Hitler joins the tiny German Workers' Party (*Deutsch Arbeiterpartei*) in Munich as member number 7
November	Hitler gives his first speech, the first of many at the Hofbrauhaus Beer hall in Munich

1920

February	The first Party office opens in the Sterneckerbräu brewery and Hitler outlines the Party program at the Hofbrauhaus in front of 2,000 people
April	The Party changes its name to the *Nationalsozialistische Deutsche Arbeiterpartei* (NSDAP, the National Socialist German Workers' Party)
October	The 'Storm Group', (*Sturmabteilung*) or SA is formed to keep order at meetings

1921

January	The NSDAP holds its first National Congress in Munich
July	Hitler emerges as the head of the NSDAP following a leadership crisis

1922

October	The SA drive communists out of Coburg, the start of violence across Germany

Nazis behind barricades they have erected on a Munich street during the Munich Beer Hall Putsch. Heinrich Himmler, who would later lead the SS, carries the flag.

1923

November	The Munich Beer Hall Putsch. The Army and the Bavarian government fail to support it. Hitler is arrested and jailed in Landsberg; the Nazi Party and SA are banned

1924

	Hitler starts work on his book *Mein Kampf* (My Struggle)
December	Hitler is released from Landsberg to find the NSDAP in ruins

1925

February	Hitler re-launches the Nazi Party at the Burgerbraukeller. *Mein Kampf* is published in the summer

1926

July	The first party rally is held in Weimar; 5,000 attend

1927

May	Hitler is allowed to speak in public in Bavaria and Saxony
July	The first Nuremberg Rally attracts 30,000

1928

May   The Nazis win twelve seats in the Reichstag; membership reaches 100,000

December   The second volume of *Mein Kampf* is published

1930

September Nazis win 107 seats and become the second largest party in the Reichstag; by now the SA is larger than the Regular Army

1931

January   The Nazi Party move its headquarters to the Brown House in Munich

1932

March   Hindenburg defeats Hitler in the Presidential elections; the SA are banned when it is rumoured that they are planning a *Putsch*; the ban is lifted in June

April   Hindenburg is re-elected in a second Presidential election but the Nazis gain Prussia in the State elections

Hindenburg and Hitler. The German upper class thought that they could control him.

July   The Nazis become the largest party in the Reichstag with 230 seats

August   Hindenburg refuses to hand over the chancellorship to Hitler

December   Schleicher is appointed Chancellor

1933

January   Schleicher resigns and Von Papen agrees to be Vice-Chancellor with Hitler as Chancellor of a largely conservative cabinet; only three of the eleven ministries go to the Nazis

February   Hermann Göring, the Prussian Minister of the Interior, creates an auxiliary police force with 50,000 SA men

The Reichstag Fire: Hindenburg signs a decree suspending civil rights and the SA arrest thousands of the Nazis' political opponents

Von Papen.

March	The last Reichstag elections are held. The Nazis ban the communist and socialist members from the Reichstag to gain a majority; political opponents are rounded up and imprisoned in concentration camps. Hitler announces *Gleichschaltung*, the coordination of political will, and the Enabling Law giving him special powers for the next four years; the first of many laws are passed a few days later
April	Jewish staff are dismissed from the civil service, the first of many pogroms, while a boycott targets Jewish shops
May	Labour unions are disbanded and replaced by the Labour Front
July	The Nazi Party is made the only legal political party
October	The Reichstag is dissolved and Germany withdraws from the League of Nations
November	A referendum shows that 95 percent of the German people approve of the Nazis
December	A law securing the unity of the Party and the Reich is passed

Ernst Röhm, leader of the SA, was removed without recourse to law. He along with hundreds of others was murdered on Hitler's orders; a clear indication of the ruthlessness the German people, and the world, could expect under the Nazis.

1934

June	Ernst Röhm, leader of the SA and hundreds of other troublemakers are murdered during the Night of the Long Knives
August	Hindenburg dies and the office of President is abolished. Hitler becomes the sole leader, or Führer, of Germany

1935

January	Saar area returned to Germany
March	Conscription is introduced
September	Göring announces the Nuremberg laws denouncing the Jews. The swastika becomes the national flag

1936

March	German troops occupy the Rhineland
August	The Olympic Games are held in Germany, resulting in a temporary respite in the persecution of the Jews

Jews were constantly harassed from 1933 onwards.

October	Göring announces the Four-Year Plan
1937	The confiscation of Jewish businesses continues
1938	
February	Hitler becomes Minister of War and Commander-in-Chief of the armed forces
March	German troops occupy Austria in the *Anschluss*
September	The Munich Agreement hands over the Sudetenland area of Czechoslovakia to Germany in the hope of securing peace
November	*Kristallnacht*, the night of broken glass. Hundreds of synagogues

British Prime Minister Neville Chamberlain comes to an agreement with Adolf Hitler at Munich in September 1938. One year later Chamberlain had to declare war on Germany when Poland was invaded.

SS troops in action in Poland.

are burnt and over 20,000 Jews are imprisoned while dozens
are murdered

1939

March   Germany occupies Bohemia and Moravia as Proctectorates.

August   The signing of the Soviet-German non-aggression pact

September   Germany invades the western part of Poland while Russia
              invades the east. Both Great Britain and France declare war on
              Germany.

The Allied Advance Across Europe

The Allies had been in northwest Europe for over six months by January 1945. After heavy fighting in Normandy, General Eisenhower's Armies had broken out across France and quickly liberated Paris and Brussels as they swept east to the German border. Another Allied landing in southern France had pushed quickly up the Rhône Valley and linked up with the main drive. Although progress was exceeding all expectations, the advance had started to falter by the end of September, not through enemy action but mounting difficulties in keeping the front line troops supplied. As summer turned to autumn, Operation Market Garden, an attempt to cross the Rhine with airborne troops at Arnhem in Field Marshal Montgomery's sector in Holland, ended in failure and Eisenhower was forced to reconsider his options.

Bitter fighting followed as the Germans regrouped along their border and battles for Aachen, the first German city to fall, and Hurtgen Forest consumed

Autumn 1944, American troops passed through the Siegfried Line defences and into Germany.

men and supplies alike. On 16 December 1944 the Germans struck back as two Panzer Armies broke through the American lines in the Ardennes, and threatened to reach the River Meuse. For two weeks American reserves poured into Belgium as rearguards fought to hold vital crossroads at St Vith and Bastogne thus stopping the German onslaught. By the beginning of January the tide was beginning to turn, the worst was over and, as the American and British troops squeezed the Bulge out of the Allied line, Eisenhower was planning to strike deep into Germany.

The Allies had seventy-one divisions grouped in six Armies ready for action and another fourteen were due to land on the continent by the beginning of January 1945. Eisenhower's men were poised along the German border and they were able to begin clearing the Siegfried Line and the west bank of the

Field Marshal Montgomery

Rhine, confident that a vast logistical organisation would keep them supplied.

Meanwhile, the attack in the Ardennes had consumed a large part of Hitler's reserve. With the Allies poised on the borders in the west and the Russians threatening to carve across eastern Germany it was only a matter of time before Hitler's thousand-year Reich would come to an end. The end of the war and victory in Europe was in sight but there was hard fighting ahead. Hitler and the Nazis had motivated the entire German population to resist the invaders and the Allied soldiers would have to fight every inch of the way.

21 Army Group

General Crerar

Eisenhower's first objective was to destroy the German forces west of the Rhine and on 8 February First Canadian Army launched Operation Veritable, the first of a series of Allied offensives. For two weeks General Crerar's men endured harsh weather conditions and heavy resistance as they pushed southeast from Nijmegen and the Reichswald Forest towards the Rhine.

General Simpson

Field Marshal Montgomery's second attack, a drive northeast in Ninth US Army's sector to trap Germans on the west bank of the river, was scheduled to start at the same time. However, a series of dams controlling the flow of the Roer River crossing in General Simpson's sector had to be taken first. V Corps struck out through the Hürtgen Forest on 5 February and five days later seized Schwammenauel Dam before German engineers could destroy it, however, the damaged valves sent floodwaters pouring across Simpson's front for several days.

Ninth Army finally launched Operation Grenade on 23 February, taking the Germans by surprise, and by nightfall Ninth Army was firmly established on the far bank of the Roer. Simpson unleashed his armour four days later and it advanced quickly towards Düsseldorf and Wesel. The link up with the Canadians was made on 5 March and despite the delays over 36,000 Germans were killed or captured on the west bank of the Rhine. As the shattered German troops fell back across the river, they destroyed the bridges ahead of the Allies.

12 Army Group

In the centre of the Allied front General Bradley's men spent February edging through the Siegfried Line between Pruem and Saarburg and by the end of the month they were ready to advance to the Rhine. On 1 March Operation Lumberjack began as First Army and Third Army made a pincer attack, hoping to trap thousands of Germans on the west bank. First Army made rapid progress across the Erft River and headed southeast towards the confluence of the Ahr and Rhine Rivers. By 5 March the Rhine was in sight at Cologne but as Hodges' troops turned south along the river to link up with Third Army's advance northeast towards Koblenz, luck played its part on 7 March at the small riverside town of Remagen.

A spotter plane had noticed that the Ludendorff Rail Bridge was still standing but as 9th Armoured Division's task force moved through the town demolitions rocked the structure. To everyone's surprise the bridge was still standing and as Lieutenant Timmermann's GIs ran across, the news shocked both the Allied and German High Commands. By chance, rather than design, the Allies had established a bridgehead over the Rhine.

In the days that followed the Germans tried to destroy the bridge, employing saboteurs, the Luftwaffe and artillery but to no avail and by the time the bridge finally collapsed on 17 March, Bradley had five divisions on the east bank. Despite the opportunities offered, Eisenhower stuck to his original plan and ordered First Army to hold a ten-mile deep bridgehead in the hope of drawing German reserves from Montgomery's front to the north.

6 Army Group

At the southern end of the Allied line the Seventh US Army and the First French Army concentrated on straightening their frontline. By 9 February a German salient known as the Colmar Pocket had been cleared, opening the way for General Jacob Devers' advance towards the Rhine. Operation Undertone began on 15 March with Seventh Army's attack on the industrial Saar area. 12 Army Group's success meant that Third Army was able to cooperate and with a new revised plan to hand, General Patton turned south into General Patch's sector allowing Seventh Army to concentrate on breaking the Siegfried Line. Third Army advanced quickly toward Oppenheim and Kaiserslautern on the Rhine and when Seventh

Allied engineers build a bridge across the Rhine.

Army had broken free from the pillboxes and minefields across its front General Patch had soon cleared the Saar-Palatinate triangle.

The two Armies met on 20 March, having crushed the German *Seventh Army*; and the pincer movement had also forced the German *First Army* into a hopeless salient; it was only a matter of time before the entire west bank of the Rhine was in Allied hands.

General Jacob Devers' 6th Army Group held the southern sector of the Allied Rhine, between Frankfurt and the Swiss border. After battling its way to the Rhine, General Eisenhower had given Devers' Army Group two objectives during the final drive into Germany. As well as protecting 12th Army Group's right flank as it advanced into the heart of Germany, Seventh US Army and the First French Army had to seal off the routes into the Alps to stop the Nazis using the mountains to make a last stand. General Alexander Patch would advance northeast alongside Third Army's flank before turning south through Nuremberg and Munich. Meanwhile, the First French Army would attack to the south and southeast, taking Stuttgart before moving to the Swiss border and into Austria.

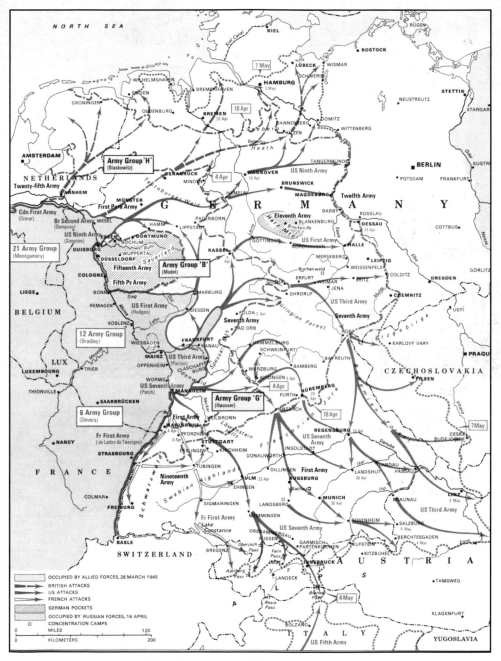

Invasion of Germany by Allied forces in the West 1945.

US Seventh Army's Advance

22 March	General Patton's Third Army crosses the Rhine south of Frankfurt
25 March	4th Armoured Division crosses the River Main at Aschaffenburg
26-28 March	XV Corps crosses the Rhine at Worms and advances to the Main
26-28 March	Task Force Baum attempts to rescue prisoners from Hammelburg Camp
26-30 March	Heavy fighting in Aschaffenburg
28 March	Seventh Army breaks out from the Main bridgehead
2-6 April	Advance through the Spessart Hills to Hammelburg
3-4 April	XV Corps battle for Wurzburg
4-12 April	VI Corps battle for Heilbronn
9-12 April	The battle for Schweinfurt
15 April	Eisenhower orders 6th Army Group to turn South towards Bavaria
18-20 April	XV Corps battle for Furth and Nuremberg
21 April	First French Army captures Stuttgart
22-25 April	Seventh Army advances to the River Danube
22 April	12th Armoured Division crosses the Danube at Dillingen
26 April	XV Corps crosses the Danube between Donauworth and Neuburg
27-29 April	The advance to Munich
29 April	XV Corps liberates Dachau Concentration Camp
29-30 April	XV Corps enters Munich
30 April	Adolf Hitler commits suicide as the Russians close in on his Berlin bunker
1-4 May	The advance to Salzburg
4 May	XV Corps reaches Berchtesgaden and Hitler's Berghof at Obersalzberg
4 May	Seventh US Army and Fifth US Army meet on the Italian frontier linking the European and Mediterranean theatres
8 May	The war in Europe comes to an end after five and a half years.

Hitler visiting troops defending the River Oder line against the Soviet advance, March 1945. He would never leave Berlin again.

A Soviet officers points to where the corpses of Hitler and his wife were burned following their suicide on 30 April 1945.

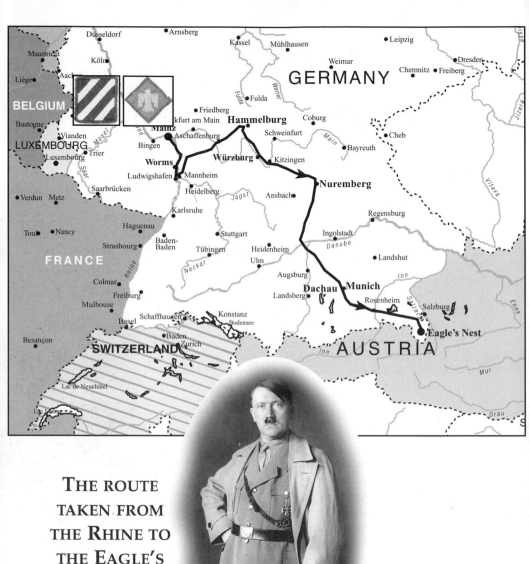

Düsseldorf • Arnsberg • Kassel • Mühlhausen • Leipzig

Maastricht • Köln • Weimar • Chemnitz • Freiberg • Dresden

Liège • Aachen • GERMANY

BELGIUM • Fulda • Fulda

Bastogne • Vianden • Friedberg • Coburg • Cheb

LUXEMBOURG • Bingen • kfurt am Main • Hammelburg • Schweinfurt • Bayreuth

Luxembourg • Trier • Mainz • Aschaffenburg

Worms • Würzburg • Kitzingen

Ludwigshafen • Mannheim

Verdun • Metz • Heidelberg • Jagst • Ansbach • Nuremberg

Saarbrücken • Karlsruhe • Regensburg

Toul • Nancy • Haguenau • Stuttgart • Ingolstadt

Strasbourg • Baden-Baden • Tübingen • Heidenheim • Danube • Landshut

FRANCE • Ulm

Colmar • Freiburg • Augsburg • Munich • Inn

Mulhouse • Landsberg • Dachau • Rosenheim • Salzburg

Basel • Schaffhausen • Konstanz • Bodensee

Besançon • Baden • Zürich • Eagle's Nest

SWITZERLAND • AUSTRIA • Mur

Lac de Neuchâtel • Drau

Lac Léman • Inn

THE ROUTE
TAKEN FROM
THE RHINE TO
THE EAGLE'S
NEST IN THIS
'PURSUIT OF
HITLER'

20

Chapter One

CROSSING THE RHINE

A S THIRD ARMY PUSHED TOWARDS THE RHINE, XII Corps commander, General Manton *Matt* Eddy, intended to withdraw the 5th *Red Diamond* Division into reserve. Major-General LeRoy Red Irwin's men had crossed twenty-two rivers during the advance across Europe and Eddy wanted them rested ready to cross the Rhine. Third Army's commander, General George *Blood and Guts* Patton had other ideas and on 21 March Eddy forwarded his plans to Irwin.

Patton was irritated by the attention lavished on General Bernard Montgomery's 21 Army Group as it prepared to cross the Rhine northwest of Düsseldorf in northern Germany. Throughout March, thousands of men and hundreds of tanks and vehicles had been directed to Montgomery's area and while the British and United States Air Forces attacked targets north of the Ruhr, two airborne divisions were placed on standby ready to drop on the far bank of the river. The attack was scheduled to start on the night of 23 March and Patton was determined to steal the show by crossing the Rhine south of Frankfurt twenty-four hours earlier. There would be no massive build-up, no aerial campaign, no airborne troops and even the artillery had to remain silent as Irwin's men slipped across under cover of darkness. Irwin protested at the lack of planning but General Eddy made it clear that Patton wanted to cross before Montgomery. He had chosen the crossing points ten miles south of Frankfurt where a range of hills afforded the

General Manton Eddy.

thirteen battalions of American artillery good observation across the river. Third Army's commander was also sure that the Germans were in a state of disarray and he wanted to establish a bridgehead before they reorganised.

Towards midday on 22 March 11th Regiment's commanding officer, Colonel Paul Black, was given the order to cross at 22:00 hours that night. Two battalions, the 1st at Oppenheim and the 3rd at Nierstein, would cross in silence in five hundred assault boats crewed by the 204th Engineer Battalion. Over 7,500 engineers waited to start work on treadway bridges and build ramps down to the shoreline for the DUKWS and ferries while Naval Unit 2 of the US Navy was on stand-by, ready to operate their small landing craft (LCVPs) on the river. Meanwhile 90th Division would create a diversion by making a feint crossing at Mainz to the south. As darkness fell across the Rhine the assault troops wondered what the German reaction would be and, more importantly, would they see dawn?

American spotter aircraft had spent the past few days searching for targets on the far bank of the Rhine but it seemed as though the German Seventh Army had gone into hiding. Seventh Army held a fifty-mile front between Wiesbaden and Mannheim and *General der Infantrie* Hans Felber's commanders had been kept busy reorganising their units since they crossed the river. Wehrkreis XII (the local military district) had made few defensive improvements on the river bank opposite Third Army and *Generalleutnant* Ralph Graf von Oriola's XIII Corps' single formation, the *159th Volksgrenadier Division*, had had insufficient time to prepare defensive positions. The *Wehrkreis* had been upgraded to an active corps but it could only muster a mixture of security detachments, students from local training schools and convalescents. General Felber was hoping that the Americans would stop along the Rhine and take time to prepare, giving him an opportunity to rally other divisions. The German situation was exactly what Patton had predicted; everything now depended on the men of 11th Regiment who were silently carrying their assault boats down to the water's edge.

The moon shone brightly over the Rhine as the two battalions paddled quietly across the Rhine. 3rd Battalion started to cross later than expected at Nierstein and Company K's commander, Lieutenant Irven Jacobs, reached the far shore half an hour behind schedule. All remained quiet as the rest of the company grounded on the shingle beach and the first group of German prisoners paddled back across the river without an escort after they were found asleep in their foxhole.

The German sentries were on their guard opposite Oppenheim, a mile to the south, and they spotted 1st Battalion's assault boats midstream. It was a tense time for Colonel Black as his GIs paddled furiously towards the east bank while bullets skimmed the water around them but only a few men were hit. Companies A and B rushed ashore and there was chaotic fighting as platoon commanders organised their men and dealt with each sentry post in turn but the outcome was never in any doubt. 11th Regiment had established a bridgehead having suffered only twenty casualties.

Wave after wave of assault boats followed the river and by midnight all three battalions were across and ready to advance to the first line of villages. So far the German reaction had been minimal and most of the sentries had been overpowered before they could raise the alarm.

The infantry fanned out, linking up the two crossings before pushing northeast towards Gross-Gerau. 3rd Battalion was held up until dawn by a large group of Germans surrounding a small airstrip along the riverbank;

The Rhine at Nierstein.

GIs hug the bottom of their craft as they cross the Rhine.

around a hundred men eventually surrendered *en masse*. As 1st Battalion advanced towards Geinsheim flares illuminated the fields and the garrison opened fire. Undeterred, the platoon leaders and squad sergeants led their men forward, firing from the hip to suppress the Germans and boost their confidence; a tactic known as 'the walking death'. The village soon fell into American hands.

5th Division's second Regiment was across by daylight and as rafts ferried tanks and tank destroyers over the river, the third crossed. The *Luftwaffe* targeted the crossing sites throughout the day, starting with an attack by twelve aircraft at first light, but damage was minimal and the engineers finished their treadway bridge by nightfall; nineteen German planes were destroyed.

General von Oriola spent all day trying to organise a counterattack but most attempts were small and uncoordinated. While groups of SS troops attacked with small arms and *Panzerfausts,* the *Volkssturm* units usually fled or surrendered at the first sign of gunfire. The main attempt to break through was made against 3rd Battalion's line in the north by a regimental-size unit of student officers and a handful of tanks and assault guns. *Feldmarschall* Kesselring, and Army Group G commander *SS-Gruppenführer* Paul Hausser ('Papa') watched as they assembled in Gross-Gerau but when *159th Volksgrenadier Division* failed to assemble in time, the order was given for the young trainees to advance at midnight. Although they infiltrated the American outposts no one entered the villages beyond. At first light seventeen American artillery battalions hammered the German-held area and while many fell back others surrendered. When *159th Volksgrenadier Division* finally attacked the southeast corner of the bridgehead, they were easily stopped.

After twenty-four hours of fighting, General Irwin was able to report that 5th Division was closing in on Gross-Gerau and its road network, prompting General Eddy to order 4th Armoured Division forward; it would cross early on the 24th and prepare to drive towards Frankfurt.

General Patton had informed General Omar Bradley of the crossing early on the 23rd but he had asked him to keep the news secret until the bridgehead was secure. Later that night he telephoned again to confirm that 5th Division was firmly established on the east bank of the Rhine; the time had come for Bradley to relay the news to the press and they were told the following morning. The announcement had the impact Patton had hoped for, snatching

Feldmarschall
Albert Kesselring.

SS-Gruppenführer
Paul Hausser.

the headlines from Field Marshal Montgomery's crossing in the north. Bradley's press release also underlined the fact that American troops were capable of crossing the Rhine at any point without the need for an aerial bombardment or the help of airborne troops; a deliberate jibe to irritate 21 Army Group's commander. The consternation caused at *Feldmarschall* Kesselring's headquarters is rather more difficult to calculate but it left Army Group G reeling as it fell back across the River Main.

Directions to Nierstein and Oppenheim

Exit Autobahn 60 at Junction 24, southeast of Mainz, and head south on Route 9 towards Oppenheim and Nierstein. There is a petrol station on the right after 1 mile, a useful fill point before you start your tour. Continue south for 7 miles into Nierstein where it is possible to stop along the waterfront. 5th Division made one of its surprise crossings here on the night of 23 March and by dawn they were established on the far bank as General Patton had hoped. Continue south through Oppenheim, the site of 5th Division's second crossing, carrying straight on at the roundabout on the far side of the village, heading for Worms.

Seventh Army's Rhine Crossing

As Seventh Army advanced to the Rhine, General Alexander *Sandy* Patch was contemplating crossing south of Mannheim, so his men would not have to fight their way through the Odenwald forest. Third Army's advance narrowed his front and although General Eisenhower had offered support of the 13th Airborne Division, General Patton's crossing called for immediate action.

General Patch recognised that crossings around Worms would allow the two Armies to link up at the earliest opportunity. His plan was for General Wade Haislip's XV Corps to cross with two divisions, 45th Division to the north of the town and 3rd Division to the south. Another two infantry divisions and a cavalry group would follow, expanding the bridgehead towards the Odenwald forest.

Present-day photo of the Germans' view of 5th Division's second crossing site at Oppenheim.

Intelligence reports believed that a large number of German divisions had escaped to the far bank of the Rhine but the majority had been decimated. *559th Volksgrenadier Division*, the only sizeable formation in the area, held

Mannheim south of the crossing sites while two under strength *Volksgrenadier* Divisions, the *216th* and *352nd*, faced XV Corps; both were short of armour, artillery and heavy weapons. Neither had had time to fortify the riverbank and mobile flak guns (20mm guns mounted on lorries and halftracks) formed the backbone of the defence. Third Army had shown that resistance might be disorganised and local patrols found only a few guards and light defences along the riverbank.

As the men prepared, the artillery moved into position and the engineers carried vital bridging equipment forward. In contrast to Patton's crossing, XV Corps' attack had a mass of artillery support but once again General Wade Haislip wanted the guns to hold their fire. He hoped to cross in silence under the cover of smoke and as zero hour approached, moonlight cast an eerie glow as the GIs moved quietly through the mist towards the river. It did, however, appear that the Germans were on their guard, and their machine guns and flak guns continued firing at the assembly areas all night.

General Wade Haislip.

45th Division's Crossing

In 45th Division's sector the men assembled in the woods around Hamm and the first wave crossed the flood dikes and pushed out into the Rhine at 02:30 hours. With bated breath the GIs huddled down in their assault boats as the small outboard motors fired into life and they prayed that they would get across alive. The Germans continued to fire blindly into the smoke and although few boats were lost during the crossing, the east bank erupted with fire as the first wave neared the shore. It was too little, too late. There were casualties but the majority of the boats beached moments later and the men clambered ashore with their rifles and submachine guns blazing. Their first priority was to secure the riverbank but the German machine gun and flak gun crews exacted a heavy toll on the waves of assault boats.

Fierce fighting erupted all along the bank as the GIs fell on the German defenders and wave after wave of boats followed. Two battalions were soon ashore in 179th Regiment's sector and within the hour Colonel Preston Murphy ordered his reserve battalion forward. By the time it was light one battalion was moving north towards Gernsheim and Third Army's bridgehead while another secured Gross Rohrheim.

The story was similar at Rheindörkheim where 180th Regiment was met by heavy fire as the boats ran aground. Colonel Everett Duvall's men stormed ashore, fanning out into the mist to silence the German outposts, but over half the assault boats in the follow up waves had been sunk by the time the east bank was secured. Despite the setbacks and heavy loss of life, the survivors regrouped and pushed on towards their first objectives. By the time it was light, Nordheim was secure and 45th Division's two bridgeheads were soon linked up.

Directions to the 45th Division's Crossing Sites

Head south from Oppenheim and turn left after 10 miles, signposted for Eich. Go straight over at the roundabout into the village and right in the centre, signposted for Giersheim ferry. Turn right for Hamm at the crossroads 21/2 miles beyond Eich and there is a parking area to the left after 400m where it is possible to walk down to the river. 179th Regiment of 45th Division crossed here on 26 March.

45th US Infantry Division 'Thunderbirds'.

Follow the narrow main street through the village and into Iberstein, taking the left turn (actually straight on) for Rheindurkheim. The road follows the river where 180th Regiment crossed; there are parking areas with paths leading down to the water's edge. Take the mandatory right in Rheindurkheim and rejoin Route 9, turning left towards Worms

3rd Division's Crossing

Either side of Worms the German sentries' suspicions grew throughout the night as 3rd Division made its final preparations. Some called for mortar fire on 7th Regiment's sector and they had destroyed several boats before they were silenced. As zero hour approached the rest of the German mortars and 20mm flak guns began searching for targets along the riverbank, hampering 10th Combat Engineer Battalion as it brought foward the assault boats. Worried that the enemy fire could seriously compromise the crossing, Major-General John O'Daniel, known as *Iron Mike* to the GIs, reluctantly ordered his own artillery to reply. The division's artillery commander, Brigadier-General William Sexton, had planned for such an emergency and a few minutes before 02:00 eleven howitzer batteries opened fire at targets on the east bank while the Corps artillery shelled other targets. As the GIs hugged the ground by their assault boats, shell bursts enveloped the east bank, 'painting the skyline a lurid red'; 10,000 rounds hit *352nd Volksgrenadier Division* in thirty-eight minutes.

30th Regiment crossed north of Worms and the assault boats of the two leading battalions were only met by sporadic fire as they forged across the river. Moments later furious fighting broke out as the GIs fell on the line of foxholes and machine gun nests covering the dike. It took several hours to mop up the German outpost line and by first light Colonel Lionel McGarr was

179th Regiment's crossing site near Hamm.

180th Regiment's crossing site on the northern outskirts of Worms.

Men storm ashore on the east bank of the Rhine.

anxious for his battalion commanders to push on towards Bürstadt before *352nd Volksgrenadier Division* counterattacked.

Disaster struck in 7th Regiment's area, south of Worms, moments before zero hour when an incendiary shell set fire to a barn in Petersau hamlet. The flames silhouetted the activities along the water's edge and the German mortars and flak guns pounded the area with shells as the GIs ran forward and pushed their boats into the Rhine. Many boats were hit and others capsized as men clambered in, while a few boats lost power mid stream, forcing the occupants to paddle frantically through the smoke to the far bank. Machine guns and rifles opened up as the boats hit the shore but the survivors scrambled over the dike to take up the

3rd US Infantry Division 'Rock of the Marne'.

fight. Casualties had been heavy and the initial chaos had delayed 7th Regiment's crossing, but at first light Colonel John Heintges was able to report that his two battalions had secured a narrow foothold on the east bank.

As the sky grew light over the Rhine, General Haislip knew that the tables were turning in his favour. All four of his assault regiments had reached the far bank and cleared the crust of the German defences along the shore. As engineers set to work building bridges, ferries and DUKWs carried men and equipment across the river while the fighter-bombers of the United States Air Force circled overhead waiting for the infantry to identify targets. The mighty Rhine had been crossed once more.

Directions to the 3rd Division's Crossing Sites

Head south through Worms' industrial zone towards the centre of the town. The section of the river where 3rd Division's 30th Regiment crossed the river runs parallel to the road. Keep straight on through two sets of traffic lights passing the twin towers of Rhienbröcke (Rhine Bridge) to the left.

German engineers demolished the bridge in March 1945 before the Americans arrived. 3rd Division built a treadway bridge alongside and named it General Patch Bridge after Seventh Army's commander.

Turn left on to the slip road for Route 9, Mannheim, after 1/2 mile and head south. After 4 miles turn right onto the slip road for Bobenheim and Roxheim and turn right at the T-junction for Petersau, heading east. The small hamlet is 1 mile away, park and follow one of the footpaths down to the high flood banks at the river 500m to the east.

An incendiary shell lit up 7th Regiment's assembly area just before zero hour in Petersau and moments later the American artillery retaliated, illuminating the far bank with a continuous blur of explosions. Men pushed their boats into the river as bullets skimmed the water but while many boats were lost, 7th Regiment stormed across the river and seized a foothold on the east bank.

Pushing East from the River

Planes were constantly operating over XV Corps' sector and every twenty minutes a new flight of eight planes reported with each divisional headquarters. If no targets had appeared by the time the next flight appeared, they flew ahead to prearranged targets. On the rare occasions that the GIs were held up, the regimental commanders knew that they could rely on close air support. Artillery spotter planes were also circling overhead ready to call in the artillery batteries on the west bank.

On the ground, all fourteen of the division's Duplex Drive amphibious tanks in 45th Division's sector had made it safely across and they were ready to give the GIs close support. In 179th Regiment's sector, one of 2nd Battalion's companies moved along the riverbank to take Klein Rohrheim but the rest of the battalion came under fire as it attacked Gernsheim. One company was pinned down but another manoeuvred past the flak guns to enter the village. By nightfall Gernsheim had fallen along with a large number of prisoners.

Meanwhile, 1st Battalion found a weak spot in the German lines and it moved rapidly through the Jägersburger Woods east of Gross Rohrheim, reaching the Frankfurt-Mannheim Autobahn by the end of the day; it had advanced over five miles.

180th Regiment's 1st Battalion had been forced to withdraw in the face of withering fire from a concentration of mobile flak guns in the centre of the division's sector and Colonel Duvall called for close air support. The fighter-bombers swooped low over the river, bombing and strafing the group of farms where the guns were hidden and 1st Battalion moved forward before the dust had settled; by late afternoon fifteen mobile flak wagons had been captured.

3rd Battalion came under fire as it approached Biblis but as one company held the Germans' attention, another moved around the flank. By midday the village had been cleared and the second of 45th Division's battalions had reached the Autobahn before the end of the day.

Seventh Army reserves file across General Patch Bridge next to the ruins of Worms' historic crossing.

3rd Division pushed quickly east despite a chaotic crossing.

By nightfall all of 45th Infantry Division's infantry and support troops were across the Rhine, carried by the DUKWs and ferries, and one battalion of artillery was already on the east bank. 40th Combat Engineer Battalion had lost over half of its assault boats in the crossing but replacements had helped the survivors to build a heavy treadway bridge and a floating pontoon bridge and both were nearing completion.

216th Volksgrenadier Division had been virtually wiped out by 45th Division's attack. Over 1,000 prisoners had been taken along with a large collection of machine guns, *panzerfausts* and small arms; 37 flak guns (including sixteen 88mms) and three 105mm howitzers had also been captured or destroyed. General Robert Frederick was also able to report that his men had cleared an area eight miles wide, and in places, eight miles deep.

3rd Division had secured a foothold on the east bank by dawn but the delays caused by the early confusion had allowed *352nd Volksgrenadier Division* to regroup. Only fifteen of 756th Tank Battalion's twenty-one DD Shermans had followed the infantry across the river, the others had sunk in midstream or floundered in the mud along the shoreline and the rest of General O'Daniel's armour had to be ferried across.

The Germans defended many of the villages in 3rd Division's sector until nightfall.

In 30th Regiment's sector 2nd Battalion eventually cleared Hofheim after the Germans withdrew to Bürstadt. Colonel McGarr knew that the town would be heavily defended and he was waiting for the DD tanks to arrive when 200 German infantry, supported by tanks and mobile flak wagons, counter-attacked. Company F took the brunt of the attack but while the GIs held the infantry at bay, the antitank-platoon stalked the vehicles with bazookas and captured *Panzerfausts* until the Germans withdrew. As 2nd Battalion regrouped, 1st Battalion came under heavy fire as it attacked Bobstadt. This time it was possible to outflank the village and no one escaped.

3rd Battalion found 500 infantry supported by tanks and anti-aircraft guns (both mobile and static) waiting for them in Lampertheim. Yet again the battalion commander made an outflanking manoeuvre but this time the Germans were waiting. As one company attacked, a second was met by a strong counter-attack as it moved around the town. An observation plane circling overhead answered Lieutenant Gerald Mehuron's calls for help, directing artillery salvoes all around the beleaguered US infantry. The third company's blocking position astride Bürstadt road was also attacked as the Germans tried to break through but the infantry held their positions, accounting for two tanks with bazookas, as Lieutenant Eldon North led the Cannon Company forward to knock out a battery of 88mm guns.

In 7th Regiment's sector 3rd Battalion was advancing towards the southern outskirts of Lampertheim when *352nd Volksgrenadier Division* launched yet another counter-attack. Infantry, supported by self-propelled guns and mobile 20mm flak wagons, hit the battalion's flank, but Sherman DD tanks and artillery fire drove them off. The battalion spent the afternoon engaged with infantry and four panzers guarding a factory complex in Viernheimer woods. By nightfall *352nd Volksgrenadier Division* was exhausted and the Lampertheim garrison was withdrawing to safety as 7th Regiment advanced towards the Autobahn.

On the south flank 1st Battalion was engaged at Sandhofen all day as huge 128mm anti-aircraft guns on the outskirts of Mannheim shelled the GIs.

Panzergrenadiers prepare to counter-attack.

Another German counter-attack is repulsed.

General O'Daniel urged Colonel Heintges forward but the battle dragged on through the night until 2nd Battalion joined the fray and stormed the village with the help of Sherman DD tanks. They found SS troops barricaded in many of the buildings and as artillery and mortar shells rained down, machine-gun teams and snipers fought for each building. The final pockets of resistance did not fall until midnight.

A burning barn lit up the Rhine at Petersau. The river bank today.

Thousands of prisoners were collected in Worms' main square.

Tanks roll across the Rhine ready to exploit Seventh Army's bridgehead.

While the rest of the division pushed east, 15th Regiment was given the task of securing an island in the centre of 3rd Division's sector where a number of German anti-aircraft guns were trapped. The crews had refused to surrender and they continued to fire at the engineers, halting bridging operations across the Rhine for several hours. The leading company attacked as soon as it crossed the river and forced its way across the narow bridge linking the island to the mainland; by nightfall it had captured seven flak guns.

By midnight General O'Daniel was able to report that his men had advanced over five miles from the river and although his men still had to capture the final objective, *352nd Volksgrenadier Division* had expended its reserves. They had also linked up with 45th Division's bridgehead to the north, expanding the American hold on the east bank of the Rhine to a width of thirty miles and over 2,500 Germans had surrendered (XV Corps casualties were 42 killed and 151 wounded). There was no time to lose as Seventh Army set about catching up with Third Army.

Captured Germans on their way to the cages.

The time was ripe for a quick drive to the River Main and into the heart of southern Germany and General Patch had already transferred 12th Armoured Division, nicknamed the *Hellcats*, to XV Corps and General Roderick Allen's men were ready to live up to their slogan *Speed is the password*.

General Roderick Allen, commander of 12th Armoured Division.

Directions along the East Bank

Head west out of Petersau, turning left after 1 mile and drive south along Route 9. Take the second slip road onto Autobahn 6 after 1½ miles, signposted for Mannheim, and head east. Leave the Autobahn at the next junction, turning left at the end of the slip road, and head north across 3rd Division's bridgehead.

Follow Route 44 though Lampertheim, where German troops counter-attacked 7th Regiment, and Bürstadt, where 30th Regiment was engaged in a fierce battle. 352nd Volksgrenadier Division collapsed when the two towns had fallen, leaving the way open for a rapid advance to the Odenwald, the wooded hills to the east.

Continue north bypassing Biblis and drive through the centre of Gross-Rohrheim and Klein-Rohrheim before following the bypass around Gernsheim. The line of villages formed 216th Volksgrenadier Division's main line of defence and 45th Division experienced heavy fighting in all of them. Continue north and 7 miles beyond Gernsheim turn right onto Route 26 heading for Darmstadt.

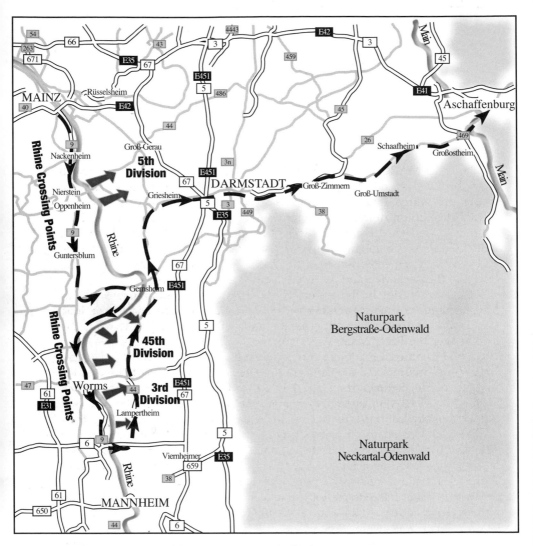

The Rhine crossing and the road to Aschaffenburg.

Chapter Two

THE BATTLE FOR ASCHAFFENBURG

O N 25 MARCH 4TH ARMOURED DIVISION'S Combat Command B headed east for Aschaffenburg with 37th Tank Battalion and 10th Armoured Infantry Battalion leading. At Grossostheim Lieutenant-Colonel Creighton Abrams split his command into three task forces, and the columns approached the Main River west and south of Aschaffenburg. The main column was engaging German troops in Babenhausen by mid morning and although the fight was one-sided, they had alerted Major Lamberth, leader of the Aschaffenburg garrison, before they were overrun.

At noon, sentries in the towers of the city's main building, the Schloss Johannisburg, noticed movement on the Babenhausen road and before long they could see the column of Shermans and halftracks heading towards the bridge over the River Main. As Company A's leading Sherman slowed to a crawl and rammed a roadblock aside, the far bank erupted as anti-tank guns, *panzerfausts*, mortars and machine guns opened fire. It was suicide to continue and the column commander ordered the crew to withdraw while he organised artillery support. The American reaction was exactly what the Germans had expected. As the column retired to a safe distance the bridge erupted in a cloud of debris as two spans collapsed into the river below. The main road into Aschaffenburg was blocked. To the south, 37th Tank Battalion's D Company, headed for Niedernberg and although the M5 light tanks had moved quickly, they found that a second road bridge had also been destroyed.

Abrams' final chance to cross the Main lay with the centre column and 10th Armoured Infantry Battalion's commander, Lieutenant-Colonel Harold Cohen. Cohen was aware that a single-track railway bridge was still standing at Nilkheim but as 37th Tank Battalion's Company B closed in, the German engineers were putting the final touches to their work.

The bridge commander, *Oberleutnant* Paul Kell, had prepared the circuits and explosives but the charges had still not arrived. Following an accident earlier that month, where a bomb had prematurely set off detonation charges wired to a bridge near Cologne, bridge commanders were ordered to store the explosives at a safe distance until orders came from above. The arrangement worked well when the engineers had plenty of notice, however, Combat

The view facing Colonel Cohen's men as they crossed Nilkheim bridge.

Command B's advance had been so rapid that *Oberleutnant* Kell had received the warning too late. He was still waiting for the detonators when the Americans arrived.

As tanks and halftracks fanned out along the riverbank and gave supporting fire, Colonel Cohen ordered his reconnaissance platoon to cross the bridge. The GIs ran along the timber decking under heavy fire, cutting wires and pushing explosives into the river, as they dodged from girder to girder. Others dived into the river below to cut explosives from the bridge piers. 10th Armoured Infantry Battalion was across the River Main and as the Germans fell back before them, the GIs spread out to form a small bridgehead. The rest of the battalion crossed on foot while the engineers made sure the bridge was safe for their halftracks and tanks to cross.

German observers in Schloss Johannisburg spotted movement across the Nilkheim Bridge shortly after midday and reported the situation to the town commander. The news came as a complete shock; the Wetterau-Main-Tauber Line had been compromised. Cohen's men quickly entered Bischberg and Erbig, seizing the low hills overlooking the bridge, scattering poorly organised German counter-attacks. By mid-afternoon the bridgehead was over a mile deep and over two miles wide.

Directions to the River Main

Drive straight through Griesheim and across the motorway, entering Darmstadt after nine miles. Following signs for Route 26, Aschaffenburg, through the town centre, make a right turn into Neckarstrasse using the filter lane. Take the first left

The villages between the Rhine and the Main have changed little since 1945.

Nilkheim Railway Bridge was wired with explosives when Combat Command B approached.

(for Aschaffenburg), crossing the tramlines into Hugelstrasse. After passing through a short tunnel, turn left and then immediate right onto the dual carriageway signposted for Route 26, Dieburg.

Take the exit for Route 45 and Gross-Umstadt after 10 miles and turn right at the end of the slip road. At the crossroads after 2 miles, turn left at the traffic lights for Grossostheim, joining the route of the 4th Armoured Division's task force as it headed for the Nilkheim railway bridge. The road winds its way across wooded hills and through villages that have hardly changed since March 1945; only the tanks and halftracks filled with GIs are missing.

After 2 miles turn left at the T-junction beyond Richen and then right at the far side of Klein-Unstadt, signposted for Grossostheim. Heading straight on through Kleestadt and Schlierbach, take the first exit at the roundabout on the outskirts of Schaafheim and carry straight on at the roundabout at the far side of the village for Grossostheim. There are wonderful views of the Spessart hills beyond the River Main; Aschaffenburg is to the left, in the distance.

Go straight on at the traffic lights into Grossostheim after 2½ miles, the village where General Patton and General William Hoge informed Colonel Abrams of their plans to rescue prisoners of war from Hammelburg camp. Turn left at the T-junction in the centre of the village and follow the main road as it makes a sharp right. Turn right at the T-junction beyond the village and cross over the autobahn.

Look out for a small concrete bridge over the road as you enter Nilkheim (2 miles beyond the autobahn) and take the first right into Mainwiesenweg after 200m. Turn first right to find Nilkheim Railway Bridge and a parking area.

A GI tries to spot an elusive sniper in the distance.

A race against time developed as Lieutenant-Colonel Abrams moved his men across to the east bank of the Main while the German attacks grew fiercer. On hearing the news, German Seventh Army commander's *General der Infantrie* Felber visited Aschaffenburg and gave orders to eliminate the bridgehead as soon as possible. Every available man and tank would be sent to defend the city; Aschaffenburg had to be held at all costs.

Combat Command B advanced north as it began to grow dark and made its first attack on Schweinheim, the suburbs east of the city where officer cadets stationed in the barracks were waiting for them. Several tanks were knocked out and after fierce hand-to-hand fighting, Abrams ordered Cohen to withdraw his men. Tanks were vulnerable in built up areas and 4th Armoured Division had done all it could; it was time for an infantry division to take over. The area was also due to be handed over to US Seventh Army at midnight and fresh troops were moving up to take over the bridgehead. Although the changeover made tactical sense, it would take time, time that the Germans would use to reinforce Aschaffenburg.

The second day at Aschaffenburg was a stand off, as the Americans and Germans reorganised their lines and *General* Felber was moving reserves

GIs shelter before advancing into the ruined city.

forward to reinforce the city's garrison as 4th Armoured Division prepared to hand over its sector. Colonel Abrams had been ordered to disengage and secure the perimeter around the bridge, leaving patrols to probe the German defences in Schweinheim. They found plenty.

413th Replacement Division joined Seventh Army during the night and *36th Volksgrenadier Division* was moving towards the southern side of the bridgehead; elements of *XIII Korps* and *256th Volksgrenadier Division* were also heading towards Aschaffenburg. *Feldmarschall* Wilhelm Keitel had also sent men to the city with orders to fight to the last. As SS-*Obersturmbannfuhrer* Wegener took command of Festung Aschaffenburg, *Stapsapotheker* Stumpf, a district Judge from Berlin, set up a military court in the city. Anyone suspected of desertion or failing to do his duty would be immediately court-martialled and, if found guilty, executed. The message from *OKW* was clear; Aschaffenburg must be held.

At midnight on 26 March an American Task Force of over fifty vehicles and 300 soldiers broke through the German lines at Schweinheim and headed into the night. Hardly anyone apart from the commanding officer, Captain Abraham Baum and his superior officers knew that the column was heading towards Hammelburg Camp to rescue hundreds of American prisoners of war. (The account of Task Force Baum's raid is covered in the next chapter.) Few Germans realised that a sizable force had broken through their lines and Seventh Army would not learn of its existence until the tanks passed close to its headquarters several hours later.

27 March was a day of changing responsibilities for both sides. As *416th Division* took over the north side of the bridgehead, *36th Volksgrenadier Division* moved into line south of Schweinheim. Although troops were constantly arriving in the area, many came from training schools and replacement depots. They were poorly armed, with a little experience and the German commanders struggled to organise the assortment of units.

Meanwhile, the Americans were experiencing their own difficulties. Combat Command B was pulling back across the Main to make way for the infantry. An infantry battalion and a company of Shermans from 26th Infantry Division covered the withdrawal as 45th Division moved towards the bridgehead.

Colonel Walter O'Brien's 157th Regiment would cross first and 3rd Battalion was ordered to move to Nilkheim Bridge during the morning. Lieutenant-Colonel Felix Sparks' orders were vague, but he was to clear the high ground beyond the river, however, his orders gave the impression that Schweinheim had already been taken. He knew nothing of Task Force Baum and the raid on Hammelburg and had only been given an ambiguous warning about American tanks operating in front of his position.

Colonel Sparks reached the unguarded bridge at 14:00 hours and he could see no sign of friendly troops on the far bank. A single platoon crossed while the rest of the battalion waited and they eventually found 26th Division's men under heavy attack. Sparks discovered the truth about the situation in Schweinheim when he located their commanding officer; the Germans still held the suburbs and they were fighting for every building.

LXXIII Korps took over responsibility for the Aschaffenburg front on 28 March and found over 5,000 soldiers defending the city. It was an impressive number but they were poorly organised. The mixture of units and a lack of communications made it virtually impossible to coordinate counter-attacks. Tanks, anti-tank guns, mortars and artillery were in short supply and the German commanders could expect little help from the *Luftwaffe*.

The area Nazi leader, *Kreisleiter* Wohlgemuth, had already ordered the women, children, elderly and the sick out of the city to reduce the strain on his limited resources. The remaining 3,500 civilians huddled in cellars were ordered to help the soldiers in any way they could:

Whoever remains in the city belongs to a battle group, which will not know any

GIs edge forward warily through the ruins.

selfishness but will know only unlimited hatred for this cursed enemy of ours. They will know only complete sacrifice for the Führer and the nation. Day and night we will work. We will commit all our power to do the enemy the greatest possible damage because we know that Germany will live if we are prepared to give our lives.

Kampfkommandant Major Lamberth had also issued his own announcement to the town's *Volkssturm*, making it clear what he expected from them:

The fortress of Aschaffenburg will be defended to the last man. As long as the enemy gives us time, we will prepare and employ our troops to our best advantage. This means fight, build barriers, erect dugouts and get supplies! As of today, everyone is to give everything to the last. I order no one shall rest more than three hours out of twenty-four. I forbid any sitting around or loafing. Our belief is that it is our mission to give the cursed enemy the greatest resistance and to send as many as possible of them to the devil.

Later that night *Kampfkommandant* Lamberth received a Teletype message from OKW headquarters reinforcing his instructions; the men in Festung Aschaffenburg were to 'fight to the last cartridge'.

LXXIII Korps' first priority was to sever the Americans' link to the west bank and it had ordered *36th Volksgrenadier Division* to seize the railway bridge. However, the division was still moving towards the bridgehead and it would be over twenty-four hours before it was ready to attack.

As the Germans prepared for a long fight, the rest of 157th Regiment crossed the river as Me109 fighter planes strafed the bridge. Meanwhile, American fighter-bombers and artillery pounded Schweinheim as a company of Shermans 191st Tank Battalion and a company from 645th Tank Destroyer Battalion moved into position, joining 157th Regiment's attack on the suburb. 2nd Battalion suffered heavy casualties along the river bank and Company F was hit by machine-gun fire in Obernauer Kolonie while *panzerfausts* kept the tanks at bay. On the Regiment's right, 3rd Battalion came under fire from the Wehrkreis training school where student officers were holding out. Colonel O'Brien tried to alleviate the pressure on his regiment by pushing 1st Battalion forward to link the two attacks but sniper fire brought Company C's advance to a standstill.

To the south, 179th Regiment had moved into the bridgehead and Colonel Preston Murphy's men had spent the afternoon clearing Obernau, pushing onto the high ground on the east side of the bridgehead. The only highlight of the day came with the discovery of a warehouse full of liquor. Before long virtually every soldier had a bottle stashed in his pack, ready to celebrate when the battle was over; they faced a long wait.

Throughout the night the civilians worked alongside the soldiers, building barricades, fortifying buildings and distributing ammunition and supplies. Everyone in the town was expected to fight and *Kampfkommandant* Lamberth demonstrated what would happen to anyone who did not comply with his

Tanks and tank destroyers had to reduce each building to rubble.

orders. A *Wehrmacht leutnant* was accused of *fahnenflucht* (fleeing the flag) and had been quickly convicted and condemned to death by the SS Special Commission. The officer was hung from a lamppost in the centre of the town and a sign around his neck warned others what the penalty was for desertion.

In Schweinheim the officer candidates had barricaded themselves inside Bois-Brule Kaserne on the riverbank, ready for 157th Regiment's next attack. It came at dawn but for the second day running, 2nd Battalion failed to make any headway and the Shermans were forced to blast each building apart before the GIs could advance. 3rd Battalion's leading companies reached the first line of buildings but as they set about clearing them, the reserve company was cut to pieces moving forward; all its officers and 100 men were killed or injured in a few minutes. The artillery and mortars did their best to suppress the Germans while the survivors withdrew to safety.

Colonel O'Brien committed Lieutenant-Colonel Ralph Krieger's 1st Battalion to the centre of his attack and M36 tank destroyers of 645th Battalion followed. They targeted each building in turn, reducing them to blazing ruins and when a German observation post was spotted in the Catholic Church, the tank destroyers fired twenty-five rounds into the spire and brought it crashing to the ground.

Fighting raged throughout the day but by nightfall 157th Regiment had made little progress. Colonel O'Brien had no reserves and his battalions had suffered high casualties while 141st Tank Battalion had already lost two Shermans in the rubble.

45th Division was severely hampered by its reliance on the narrow Nilkheim railway bridge and Major-General Frederick was pushing 120th Engineer Combat Battalion to complete a treadway bridge (it would not be finished until 2 April). In the meantime, the military police operated a one-way system on the bridge while 831st and 832nd DUKW Truck Companies ferried men and supplies across the river. Despite the traffic problem, the whole division was across by nightfall and while 179th Regiment engaged *36th Volksgrenadier Division*, 180th Regiment extended the bridgehead to the south.

After a long day deploying south of Schweinheim, *36th Volksgrenadier Division* was finally ready to attack the east side of the bridgehead. It struck at midnight and, following a short bombardment, the German infantry and tanks rolled through 179th Regiment's lines. *87th Volksgrenadier Regiment* advanced towards Obernau while *165th Volksgrenadier Regiment* attacked Erbig but Colonel Murphy's men quickly recovered from the shock. The *Volksgrenadiers* soon found that tanks and anti-tank guns were blocking the few roads in the area and they started to withdraw. The advantage shifted in the Americans' favour when it became light and by midday *36th Volksgrenadier Division* was back on its start line. It was the last major German attack.

While 179th Regiment reorganised its positions, 157th Regiment continued to advance slowly into Schweinheim and although low cloud grounded air support for most of the day, artillery support had increased to ninety guns. Block by block and room by room the GIs edged forward and with the help of M5 light tanks, 3rd Battalion reached the Artillery Barracks and the main road through the suburb. Colonel O'Brien had also moved two of 1st Battalion's companies into the woods on his right flank, cutting off the Germans' escape route to the east. 465 prisoners were taken, including many Hungarian soldiers and teenagers from the *Volkssturm*, who had been forced to fight by their SS officers and NCOs.

After *36th Volksgrenadier Division* failed to capture the Nilkheim Bridge, *LXXXII Korps* made two desperate attempts to destroy it, using frogmen armed with satchel charges. On the first night the men were unable to find a safe way to the riverbank but on the second night they entered the water and began swimming upstream; they were soon spotted by patrols and killed.

By the last day of March 1945 45th Division had been fighting continuously for five days and there was no sign of the Germans surrendering. Colonel O'Brien's men were exhausted but 157th Regiment was unable to hand its sector over to fresh troops. 2nd Battalion was pinned in front of the Pioneer Barracks, along the riverbank, and 3rd Battalion was trying to clear the Artillery and Bois-Boule Barracks. However, O'Brien was determined to break the deadlock and 1st Battalion was clearing Hill 347 in the hope of sweeping around the north side of Schweinheim.

The battle intensified as the American guns pounded the barracks along Wurzberger Strasse; the German mortars replied, firing over 1,000 rounds during the day. With clear skies over the town, the air attacks continued unabated and the American planes dropped over 100 tonnes of bombs and fired over 300 rockets and 200,000 rounds of ammunition into the blazing buildings.

With American troops moving in from every side and another 680 prisoners taken, General Frederick decided it was time to offer surrender terms. At noon a small Piper Cub observation plane flew over the town and Captain Anse Spears dropped a note into the German headquarters in Schloss Johannisburg. There was no reply and as a final act of defiance, the Germans sent a Tiger II and a captured Sherman onto Schweinheim's main street. The two tanks caused consternation amongst the GIs until their bazookas and tanks had disabled the Sherman, the Tiger II withdrew with engine trouble.

155mm howitzers were needed to blast open the walls of the Pioneer Barracks.

As dawn broke on 1 April, it was obvious that time was running out for the Germans in Aschaffenburg; ammunition, water and food were all in short supply. 157th Regiment's air and artillery support was as effective as ever, driving Lamberth's men underground into the ruined cellars where they waited for the next American attack.

2nd Battalion was still fighting along the riverbank, but the Shermans' 75mm guns could not penetrate the Pioneer Barracks' thick walls. Colonel O'Brien obtained two huge 155mm self-propelled Long Tom howitzers and as they crawled forward, they blasted the walls apart while the GIs followed close behind. Half of the complex was in American hands by mid afternoon and 300 prisoners had been taken. The German officers commanding the rest of the barracks sought permission to withdraw but Lamberth replied by sentencing them to serve in the front line. The sentence meant nothing. The Americans were already moving through the rest of the Pioneer Barracks as the officers fought alongside their men.

In Schweinheim, 3rd Battalion's first attack on the Artillery Barracks was repulsed and Colonel Sparks withdrew his men while the tanks fired phosphorous shells into the cellars in an attempt to smoke the Germans out. A second attack managed to reach the building and the GIs fought from room to room, killing and capturing over one hundred men, many of them convalescing soldiers. Sparks' men then turned their attentions to the Bois-Brule Barracks across Wurzburger Strasse and as one company cleared the high ground overlooking the buildings, the rest were engaged in another round of fierce fighting. It was cleared by nightfall after every man in the barracks had either been killed or wounded. The officer cadets had done their utmost to carry out Lamberth's orders. Altogether over 1,000 prisoners had been taken across the city, leaving only around 800 fighting on in isolated pockets.

On the flanks of Aschaffenburg, US Seventh Army was sealing the exits from the town. As 157th Regiment's 1st Battalion pushed northeast cutting the roads through Hallbach, Goldbach and Hoesbach, 44th Division was blocking off the escape routes northwest of the city. The two met the following afternoon, completing the circle around the devastated town. Although *Kampfgruppe Lamberth* was trapped, the political leaders had managed to slip away earlier in the day.

With no communications or means of supplying his men, Lamberth was starting to lose control over his outlying commands and one by one they were either destroyed or surrendered. The officers in the Pioneer Barracks overruled their leader's orders and abandoned the complex, withdrawing into the town with 400 men. By mid afternoon on 2 April 2nd Battalion had cleared the area and it was advancing along the riverbank into the heart of the city. After its tough fight for Schweinheim, 3rd Battalion was able to make good progress through Fasanerie Park to the east while a battalion from 44th Division cleared

White flags hanging from the windows of Schloss Johannisburg signified the end of the siege.

a bunker complex on Kappellenberg, (known as Hill 214) north of the town. Lamberth was becoming increasingly isolated in Schloss Johannisburg.

As the attack was renewed at first light on 3 April, a captured American officer guided *7th Volkssturm Company*'s commanding officer into 157th Regiment's headquarters. The time had finally arrived to start surrender negotiations and although Colonel O'Brien called off his attacks, he was in no mood for negotiating with a junior officer, he wanted to speak to the garrison's commander. Two interpreters escorted the officer into Schloss Johannisburg under a white flag where they found Lamberth waiting for them. He was not amused to see the two interpreters and although he agreed to hang white flags from the windows of the building (the only reliable method of communication left open to him) Lamberth refused to surrender to them. Colonel O'Brien was anxious to bring the fighting to a close and he sent Colonel Sparks to meet the defiant commandant. Lamberth and Sparks spent the rest of the morning touring the ruined town contacting German strongpoints and by late afternoon on 3 April the battle for Aschaffenburg was over.

1,600 Germans had been killed or wounded and although 3,500 had been captured, they had held the Americans at bay for ten days, causing hundreds of casualties. It had been a final defiant act of the Third Reich and illustrated the iron grip that the Nazi Party and the SS could exert over the soldiers and civilians. The war in Germany would be over in four weeks but if other towns had followed Aschaffenburg's example, it could have taken months and a fearful price in lives.

Directions through Aschaffenburg

Return to the main road and turn right. Pass under one river bridge and turn right across Willingisbrücke after 1¹/₂ miles; Aschaffenburg's landmark building, the Schloss Johannisburg stands on the far bank. 4th Armoured Division's second Task Force came under heavy fire as it started to cross the bridge and as the tanks and halftracks withdrew, the German engineers demolished the structure.

Follow Löherstrasse into the city, turning right at the first roundabout after 1/4 mile and left at the second roundabout signposted for Wurzburg. The road turns right by Sandkirche Church; turn right onto Wurzbergerstrasse at the next roundabout, signposted for Route 8 and Hallbach. The road climbs out of the city through Schweinheim and the barrack area where 45th Division fought against the German officer cadets. The original barracks are near the bottom of the hill while those built in the 1930s line the road higher up the slope. Take the left fork at the third roundabout after two miles and head into Hallbach to follow the route of the Hammelberg raid.

Barrack buildings still line the main road through Schweinheim.

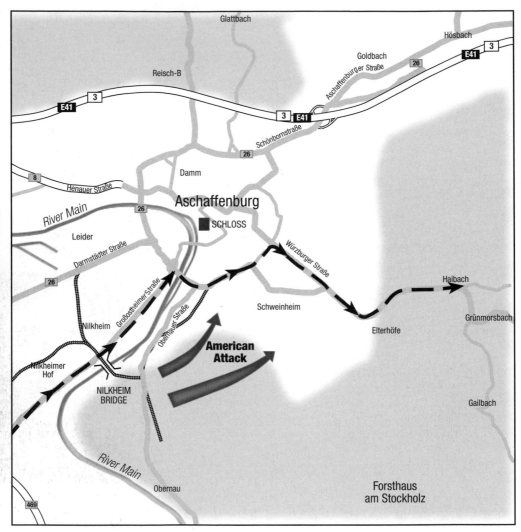

The route through Aschaffenburg.

Chapter Three

THE HAMMELBURG RAID

AMMELBURG CAMP was built for the Bavarian Army in 1895 and it had served as a prisoner of war camp in the First World War. After years of neglect, the expanding German Army returned under the leadership of *Oberst* Richard Hoppe and training once again resumed.

Two POW camps were added during the war years to guard officers and other ranks. Commander *Generalmajor* Günther von Goeckel commanded OFLAG XIII-B, the officers' camp, and by March 1945 there were two separate compounds; *Hauptmann* Fuchs' compound held American officers while *Hauptmann* Kempf ran the Serbian compound. STALAG XIII-C housed NCOs and other ranks in wooden barracks and *Oberst* Westmann had split his command into three compounds, separating the British and Commonwealth soldiers and the American soldiers; Soviet prisoners accounted for the largest number. While the officers did not have to work, the men were often assigned duties in the nearby villages.

Around 300 American officers arrived at the camp on 11 January 1945 and by the end of the month the number had increased to over 450 officers; the majority had been captured during the Battle of the Bulge.

The officers lived in seven stone barrack buildings, with around 200 men crowded into each block. Coal for the small stoves was in short supply and at the insistence of Colonel Charles Cavender, the senior American officer, work details were eventually allowed to collect fuel. There were no washrooms and the toilet facilities were inadequate for the

Generalmajor Günther von Goeckel.

large numbers of men. Men continued to wear their uniforms but they were soon in rags and jackets, sweaters and extra socks were in short supply. With no mail to look forward to, morale plummeted as the men struggled to keep warm and healthy. Bread and ersatz coffee formed the staple diet, with barley soup and vegetables served once a day, but the officers were allowed to buy extra vegetables from the canteen if they were available. However, rations were halved as the weeks passed and by the end of March many officers were suffering from malnutrition. Medical facilities were rudimentary and Major Albert Berndt, the Senior Medical Officer, was kept busy looking after the sick, many suffering from wounds received in battle. American Red Cross packages never reached the camp but the Serbian officers often shared what little they had with their allies, saving many lives.

Tensions between the Americans and their guards increased when it became clear that the Ardennes Offensive, Hitler's last-ditch attempt to break through the American lines, had failed. The prisoners were confined to barracks for long periods as the number of Allied bombing raids increased and on two occasions officers were shot for failing to observe the strict confinement rules.

As the Russians advanced into Poland, many prison camps had to be evacuated and on 21 January 1945 1,282 American officers and 109 enlisted men left OFLAG 64 in Szubin, Poland, amongst them was Lieutenant-Colonel John K Waters, General Patton's son-in-law. Waters had been captured in Tunisia on 14 February 1943 and he had been taken to the Polish Camp shortly

afterwards. The officers headed south to a new destination deep inside Germany but three officers managed to escape during the march and eventually they reached Moscow on 9 February. The news of Colonel Waters capture was reported to Washington by General John Deane, Commander of the US Military Liaison Office, and General Eisenhower informed General Patton that his son-in-law was still alive. Intelligence reports also believed that many of the prisoners were being moved to Hammelburg.

Lieutenant-Colonel John K Waters.

Their assessment proved to be correct and on 9 March 423 officers (including Lieutenant-Colonel Waters) and 67 enlisted men reached OFLAG XIII-B after six weeks on the march. Colonel Paul Goode took over as Senior American Officer and set to work organising the new arrivals. Although morale rose, the large number of new arrivals put an extra strain on the limited resources. Their health had suffered during the long march and although the medical officers had tried to conceal drugs and instruments the guards had confiscated most items.

On 24 March General George Patton called XII Corps Headquarters and gave General Manton Eddy instructions to prepare to liberate Hammelburg Camp, as soon as he had crossed the River Main. As previously noted 4th Armoured Division crossed the river south of Aschaffenburg the following day. Eddy believed that it was impossible for a Combat Command to penetrate seventy miles into German territory and then return safely with prisoners but early the following morning he tried to convince Patton to cancel the raid. Patton stood by his order but agreed to scale the size of the relief force down to a Task Force of around fifty vehicles and three hundred men.

General Eddy reluctantly called 4th Armoured Division's Headquarters and gave Brigadier-General Hoge the news while his Chief of Staff, Brigadier-General Ralph Canine, prepared the operation details.

An early photograph of Hammelburg Camp.

General Patton later flew to XII Corps headquarters and, finding Eddy absent, notified General Hoge that he should mobilise the Task Force. He then visited Hoge's headquarters in Rossdorf to go over the final details before moving on to meet Combat Command B's leader, Lieutenant-Colonel Creighton Abrams, at Großostheim. 10th Armoured Infantry Battalion had been warned about the mission and shortly after Patton left, Captain Abraham Baum was given the go ahead; Company B would set off later that night with 37th Tank Battalion's Company B as support.

At 20:30 hours 4th Armoured Division's artillery fired a short barrage on Schweinheim as a diversion but Task Force Baum found itself embroiled in a fierce street battle as it tried to reach the Hailbach road. After a three-hour delay elements of Combat Command B came to the rescue, drawing fire from the Task Force. By midnight the column of tanks, halftracks, jeeps and 105mm assault guns was on its way into the unknown. No one knew if they would make it back alive.

German soldiers in Hailbach were taken by surprise by the sight of American armour rolling by, but a few opened fire from upper storey windows causing casualties in the halftracks below. A German civilian showed Lieutenant William Weaver, the light tank platoon commander at the head of the column the turning to Keilberg and after heading north for a short distance, they turned onto the Lohr Road and moved east into the Spessart region, an area of wooded hills and deep valleys. For the rest of the way the Task Force would be confined to a single road and Captain Baum had to hope that the Germans did not destroy one of the many bridges crossing the rivers and streams along the route.

Around 03:00 hours on 27 March the column was passing through Laufach when German sentries opened fire on the leading vehicles with *Panzerfausts*.

One of the Stuarts was damaged but the rest of the tanks opened fire with their machine guns, killing five while the rest scattered; a Sherman attempted to tow the disabled tank but it soon had to be abandoned.

Although telephone cables along the route had been cut, it was impossible to conceal the amount of noise the tanks and halftracks were making and a mile to the north sentries in Heigenbrücken alerted *Seventh Army*'s command post. *General* von Obstfelder did not have any troops close by so he ordered *Wehrkreis XIII* headquarters at Nuremberg to alert training and replacement units in its area so they could intercept Task Force Baum. Von Obstfelder did not know where the American column was heading but the poor road network limited its options. His main concern was that the Americans had broken through with a large force; the fact that it was a raid to rescue prisoners of war never crossed the General's mind. As Captain Baum's men rolled through the night along the endless forest roads, little did they know that the German forces were gathering.

Task Force Baum was confined to narrow mountain roads on the road to Hammelburg.

The German Volkssturm looked on in astonishment as tanks and halftracks rolled through their villages in the dead of night.

At the tiny hamlet of Bischborner Hof the column opened fire on a Labour Service training camp and, although the fight was a one sided affair, several GIs were hit; they would have to wait until they returned to American lines before they could be treated.

There was no shooting as the Task Force rattled through Rechtenbach but observers watched and counted the vehicles as they passed, before telephoning *Oberstleutnant* Trenk in Lohr. Despite the warning, neither Trenk nor Eduard Röß, the Nazi Party leader, could do anything to stop the column. The engineers under their command needed time to prepare the bridge over the River Main but the local *Volkssturm* failed to take action and a surprised sentry gave Captain Baum's

interpreter directions through the town as the column passed through his unlocked roadblock. (Unbeknown to the Germans, the Task Force was heading across the Lohr stream where the bridge had not been prepared for demolition.)

Even so, the Americans took no chances, indiscriminately firing at doors and windows along the narrow main street to stop snipers taking aim. Once over the Lohr stream, Task Force headed along the Main valley towards Gemünden. They had already travelled thirty miles and were over halfway to their target but with dawn approaching and the Germans alerted to their presence, the most difficult part of the journey lay ahead.

Beyond Neuendorf the column fired shots at a stationary flak-train on the tracks beside the road and then targeted a troop train parked at the Gemünden railway triangle as they rolled into Langenprozelten. Captain Baum knew that Gemünden, with its twin bridges over the Sinn and Saale Rivers, could pose a problem and he ordered the column to halt in front of the town while the reconnaissance platoon went ahead to investigate. It returned with both good

The task force drove alongside the River Main towards Gemünden.

Sherman tanks in Langenprozelten on the outskirts of Gemünden.

and bad news. Although the road and rail bridges over the Sinn River were still standing, German troops were waiting on the far side. Gemünden sat astride one of the main routes through the Spessart region and *Seventh Army* had already dispatched a company of engineers from *Pionierbataillon 46* to the town to prepare the bridges for demolition and they had already completed their task.

Unaware of the dangers, Captain Baum ordered Lieutenant Sutton's armoured infantry platoon to dismount and accompany Lieutenant Raimond Keil's platoon of Shermans forward, expecting them to sweep aside the men guarding the bridge. He was sadly mistaken. The Germans waited until the Shermans were closing in and then fired everything they had. Three tanks shuddered to a halt, while men were hit as they ran onto the bridge. Three men had been killed, and another eighteen wounded but the tragedy was far from over. As Baum watched in

Captain Abraham J Baum.

horror, the German engineers destroyed part of the structure, leaving Lieutenant Keil's tank crew and Lieutenant Sutton's platoon trapped. Thirty-seven men were taken prisoner.

With the way forward blocked, Baum needed to find another route to Hammelburg and after a German prisoner confirmed that the bridge at Burgsinn could carry the tanks, Baum decided to head north. Before leaving, Baum took steps to exact his revenge on the Gemünden garrison, requesting an air strike on the town. P-47 Thunderbolt fighter-bombers attacked the town several hours later, razing many wooden buildings to the ground.

At 4th Armoured Division's headquarters General Hoge was anxiously waiting for news. So far information had been scarce, but a weak radio transmission reporting German troops were moving to Gemünden was a sign that Task Force Baum was well on its way to Hammelburg. The last report indicated that there had been twenty casualties and four tanks had been knocked out but after that there was nothing; Task Force Baum was on its own.

The Task Force reached Burgsinn at 09:30 hours (having lost two M5A1 tanks through thrown tracks) and after taking a number of prisoners, including a general, Baum's interpreter was led to the narrow side road leading to Gräfendorf. The column came across 150 Soviet prisoners and after taking the guards captive, Captain Baum advised them to hide in the forest and wait for the American Army to liberate the area. As the tanks climbed down the steep slope and passed through Gräfendorf heading for Weickergröben, the GIs watched nervously as a Storch reconnaissance plane circled overhead. It was a sure sign that German troops would be assembling to meet them.

In fact *Wehrkreis XIII* had known Task Force Baum's objective for several hours. A map had been discovered in one of the disabled tanks left at Gemünden and Hammelburg Camp had been clearly marked. The Germans had plenty of time to formulate a plan to intercept the American column and several units were already on their way. One hundred officer cadets had left Grafenwöhr in buses, while lorries had collected another 1,300 troops from Waigolshausen railway station and were taking them to Hammelburg. Two trains had also been diverted to the town and before long *Hauptmann* Heinrich Kohl was unloading *Panzerjagerabteilung 251* and its Hetzer assault guns at the town's station. A second train was not far behind and *Nachrichten Ersatz-und Ausbildungsabteilung 10* was soon helping the local *Volkssturm* to erect barricades and fortify buildings in the town.

Captain Baum knew none of this and he was relieved when his vehicles had crossed the Fränkische Saale river in Michelau, the last bridge before Hammelburg. After losing another tank through engine trouble and then making a wrong turning into Sodenberg quarry, the column joined the Gemünden – Hammelburg road and headed towards their objective.

As the Task Force turned away from the town of Hammelburg and started

Second Lieutenant Ray Keil's knocked out tank. Captain Baum had to find another way to cross the Fränkische Saale river. Before leaving he called down an air strike on Gemünden.

to climb the hill towards the camp, *Hauptmann* Kohl's Hetzers opened fire from the outskirts of the town. Three half-tracks and two Jeeps were knocked out, but the vehicles kept moving as two Stuka dive-bombers swooped low overhead, hitting the rear of the column with their bombs.

News of the approaching column had already reached the Camp Commandant, *Generalmajor* Günther von Goeckel, and he had notified Colonel Paul Goode that the prisoners had to

Oberfeldwebel
Eugen Zoller
defended the
Gemünden bridge.

Gemünden was devasted by air strikes. This is viewed from the German cemetery.

prepare to be evacuated. The order came too late. As news of the imminent rescue operation spread, Task Force Baum pulled up outside the gates just after 16:00 hours.

After a long discussion von Goeckel realised that he had no option but to surrender and told Colonel Goode to make arrangements with Captain Baum. As Lieutenant-Colonel Waters led four brother officers towards the gate carrying the Stars and Stripes and a white flag, it seemed as though the prisoners' ordeal was over. Unfortunately, one guard had not received the message and as shots rang out, Waters fell to the ground seriously wounded. The Americans waiting outside the gate decided that it was time for action and at 18:15 hours tanks drove into the main gate, sending it crashing to the floor.

Joyous scenes followed as the prisoners crowded round their liberators, exchanging hugs and handshakes, and Baum's men did their best to hand out candy to the hungry men. Meanwhile, Captain Baum and Colonel Goode were discussing arrangements for evacuating as many men as possible before the Germans arrived. Baum had been told to expect around 600 prisoners rather than 1,500 and the two officers quickly concluded that the seriously ill would have to be left behind with the medical staff; it was a heartbreaking decision. As many wounded as possible were loaded onto the vehicles while the healthy men prepared for the long march back to American lines.

Captain Baum knew that it would be suicidal to retrace his route past Hammelburg, so Lieutenant Nutto was ordered to take four tanks and three half-tracks to find an escape route. Nutto headed south but ran into a roadblock near Bonnland and after retracing his steps found another roadblock on the north side of the training area. His investigation of roads to the west had more success and after reaching the main road at Hessdorf his group headed north towards Höllrich. Captain Baum ordered the rest of his men to follow but it was nearly midnight when the tanks and halftracks, loaded with prisoners, began to follow. Although it appeared that the escape was underway, events began to unravel at an alarming rate.

Just after midnight three squads of *Panzerjagdkommando Bartmeier* had reached the camp's main gate and *Leutnant* Bartmeier ordered one of his squads to search the military training area. It knocked out one of Baum's tanks as the Task Force headed into the Reussenburg woods. Training cadets from artillery training schools arrived soon afterwards and took up positions around the prison camp. *Kampfgruppe Demmel* soon joined them and one roadblock led by *Hauptmann* Gehrig ambushed Nutto's column at Höllrich, knocking out three tanks. It was obvious that the Task Force was surrounded and as Colonel Goode returned to the camp with most of the prisoners, Baum started to make preparations for a breakout.

At dawn one of *Panzerjägerabteilung 251*'s companies reached the camp and *Major* Eggemann took command, ordering the forces gathered there to prepare to attack. *Hauptmann* Rose had been watching the Americans from his

63

GIs move towards two disabled Sherman tanks blocking Lohr's main street.

The same view today.

observation post on Reussenburg Hill and he was able to tell Eggemann where they were assembled. With everything in place, *Hauptmann* Köhl was given orders to attack as soon as possible.

Captain Baum had decided to make a break for it, but as his officers gathered around their CO's jeep to get their orders, smoke shells exploded across the Military Training Area. The decision had come too late and German tank destroyers advanced towards Baum's position as infantry ran alongside. The attack caused consternation in the American ranks and hardly a shot was fired before Baum ordered a cease-fire and reluctantly raised a white flag. Many of the able-bodied men chose to run for it, and broke into small groups in the hope of reaching the American lines. Only thirty-five men made it. Twenty-six were killed and a similar number were injured or reported missing; 236, including an injured Captain Baum, were taken prisoner. General Patton's plan to rescue the Hammelburg prisoners had been a total failure.

The day after the raid 500 prisoners were escorted from the camp and taken by train to Nuremberg. As stragglers were returned to the camp, groups of around fifty able-bodied men at a time marched away under escort heading for *Stalag VII-A*, ninety miles to the southeast at Moosburg. The medical officers were left behind to care for the sick. On 3 April lorries started to transport them to Bad Kissingen, a hospital town to the northeast, but only a few had been moved before 14th Armoured Division entered the camp three days later and finally liberated the few remaining prisoners.

Officially the raid never happened and the death of President Roosevelt a few days later distracted the press long enough to confine it to history. Patton blamed generals Eddy and Hoge for talking him out of sending a larger force but the idea and the true purpose of the raid were firmly on his shoulders. He later said 'throughout the campaign in Europe I know of no error I made except that of failing to send a Combat Command to take Hammelburg'. The admission was no comfort to Captain Baum's men.

The subsequent advance through the Spessart Hills

14th Armoured Division, the 'Liberator' Division, had crossed the Rhine on 1 April 1945 and moved forward to join Seventh Army's drive through the Spessart Hills. Major-General Albert Smith had been given orders to clear the road through Lohr and Gemünden, seizing a bridgehead over the Main to open another route through the area. Colonel Francis Gillespie's Combat Command B (CCB) was given the difficult task of following Task Force Baum's route and, as we have already seen, he would have to contend with hills and rivers that would confine his vehicles to narrow forest roads.

On the morning of 2 April, 47th Tank Battalion, with 19th Armoured Infantry Battalion mounted on halftracks, set off across country. They were soon moving east along Reichsstrasse 26 and they had covered 75 miles by the late afternoon. Task Force Baum had passed through Lohr unmolested a few days earlier but this time, the Germans were prepared; in the words of the Divisional history, 'the drive had been like a honeymoon and the honeymoon ended at Lohr'.

Ahead of Gillespie's tanks, a Flying Court Martial, led by *Major* Erwin Helm had been roaming the area, looking for deserters while SS troops executed anyone found in a house displaying a white flag. They had also set Lohr's *Volkssturm* to work building roadblocks as stragglers poured into the town, bringing the number of soldiers to over 500. *Oberstleutnant* Wilhelm Trenk had been sent to lead the defence of the town and he had three *Sturmgeschütz* assault guns to cover the roads.

To begin with Colonel Gillespie tried to bludgeon his way through the town centre, mounting the Armoured Infantry on the tanks for protection. They did not get far. Snipers and machine guns took their toll on the GIs, while *panzerfausts* knocked out three Shermans in the narrow streets. It was suicidal to continue and after withdrawing the survivors, the division's Howitzers caused devastation among the town's timber-framed buildings.

While the artillery carried out its deadly work, Gillespie ordered 47th Tank Battalion to send its company of light tanks into the woods, to try and outflank the German strongpoints. By dawn Lohr's streets were in ruins and as 19th Armoured Infantry Battalion attacked, with 47th Tank Battalion's Shermans following, the M5A1 Stuart tanks engaged *Kampfgruppen Trenk*'s rear. Another five Shermans were knocked out in heavy fighting along the main street, but with the help of 636th Tank Destroyer Battalion's Hellcats, the Germans were eventually forced to withdraw and they fell back in disarray towards Gemünden. By the time CCB left Lohr on 3 April, it was a smouldering ruin.

A rearguard at Sackenbach made good use of three anti-tank guns to stop 47th Tank Battalion's light tanks turning the retreat into a rout and Gillespie had to call for fighter-bombers to clear the road. After regrouping, Company B's Shermans

The rockets of the Sherman Calliope tank could deliver a devastating amount of firepower.

Lohr's main street: one tank has been badly damaged and the second has accidentally driven into a building.
The same scene today.

took over the lead with the GIs on board only to find some of *Oberstleutnant* Trenk's men waiting on the hillside, covering the road with machine guns and mortars. As the men fanned out into the trees to engage the Germans, the tanks continued to crawl forward. After rounding up the rearguard the column spent the night at Nantenbach, contemplating their next objective, the soldiers longed to be out in open countryside away from the narrow valley where the river and wooded hills hemmed them in, however, there was still a long way to go. The following morning one of Company D's light tanks was disabled as it moved into Langenprozelten and yet again Colonel Gillespie was taking no chances. As the tanks regrouped, fighter-bombers paved the way for the Armoured Infantry by reducing the village to a ruin.

The German engineers had made temporary repairs to one of the river bridges, and Gillespie was anxious to take it before it could be destroyed. The troops defending the west bank had other ideas and, as artillery shells and rockets fired by a Sherman tank (*Calliope*) turned Gemünden into a blazing inferno, the GIs inched forward towards the River Sinn. Time after time they were driven back as they tried to get to the bridge, but machine guns in the houses overlooking the river covered every approach. As the last of the Germans withdrew to the east bank, the engineers destroyed the temporary span, leaving Gillespie no option but to withdraw his men. He would need to bring his own engineers forward to carry out an assault crossing.

At dawn on 5 April men of the 19th Armoured Infantry left their halftracks and climbed into assault boats, crossing the river under fire from the houses on the far bank. After clearing the first row of houses, more GIs crossed and the attack on Gemünden began in earnest. 3rd Division had sent forward a battalion to reinforce the attack and Colonel Gillespie again decided to outflank the German positions. 10th Combat Engineer Battalion began cutting trees to dam the River Main east of the town as DUKWs moved forward through the trees loaded with infantry. By slowing the flow of water, the amphibious vehicles were able to cross and they began ferrying 3rd Division's battalion across at midday while tanks gave covering fire. The attack to their rear threw the Germans into confusion and by nightfall seventy prisoners had been taken. As the GIs regrouped and rested, the engineers worked through the night to repair one of the river bridges and by dawn the road to Hammelburg was open.

CCB was put under 3rd Infantry Division's command on 6 April and General O'Daniel's next objective was the Hammelburg prisoner of war camp. While 19th Armoured Infantry Battalion secured the roads to the south and east, 47th Tank Battalion would enter the camp from the north. The Americans found German tanks waiting for them and three Shermans were knocked out at Hessdorf. Tank destroyers knocked out two of the German tanks, (they were later found to be captured Shermans from Task Force Baum) opening the road onto Hammelburg Training Area.

Prisoners gather round to welcome their liberators as an M5A1 Stuart Tank crashes through the gate.

GIs crossed the River Sinn in assault boats while Germans fired down on them from the buildings on the left.

Direction of crossing

Hundreds of Serbian officer inmates were waiting in *OFLAG XIII-B* and after the locks had been shot off the gate, a tank drove through the barbed wire fences to the sounds of cheering. Pandemonium broke out as the officers crowded around their liberators, exchanging handshakes and hugs as the GIs handed out cigarettes and candy. Seriously wounded American officers were found in the camp hospital and amongst them were Captain Baum and Lieutenant-Colonel Waters. Both were evacuated and later recovered from their injuries. The enlisted men's POW camp, *STALAG XIII-C*, was also liberated and again the American soldiers were greeted with cheers and shouts of joy as the gates were thrown open. Hammelburg camp had finally been freed.

Directions to Hammelburg

From Hallbach head east along Route 8 as it winds its way down the hill through the town. Turn left in

The main entrance to Hammelburg Camp.

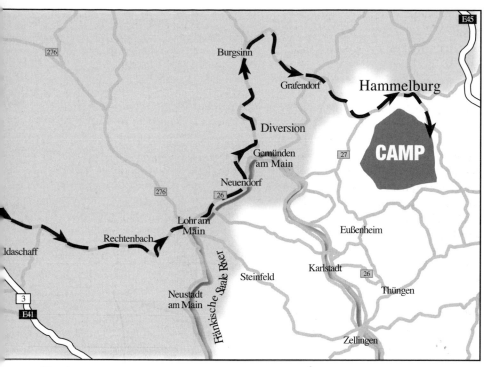

The Hammelburg Raid.

Strassebessenbach at the bottom of the hill, heading north through Keilberg, and after 3 miles turn right, signposted for Laufach. Cross the autobahn and the railway, then turn right at the roundabout for Lohr. Route 26 twists and turns through thick woods as it follows deep valleys and climbs steep hills past Rothenbuch and Rechtenbach to Lohr, 18 miles away.

The centre of Lohr has been pedestrianised and it is advisable to park in front of the railway station if you wish to visit the old town. Turn right at the traffic lights and the car park is on the left. Task Force Baum passed unmolested along Hauptstrasse during the early hours of 27 March but when 14th Armoured Division entered the town five days later, Kampfgruppen Trenk was waiting. Many of the wooden buildings were burnt to the ground in the battle that followed; they have been rebuilt in their original style.

Return to your car and carry straight on across the level crossing, keeping on the main road as it bends to the left and follow the one-way system around the town. Turn left at the traffic lights, signposted for Gemünden and after the next crossroads, turn right to join the road to Gemünden. The road weaves its way along the Main valley as it passes Sackenbach, Nantenbach, and Langenprozeltzen to Gemünden 9 miles away.

Carry straight on at roundabout on the approaches to Gemünden. To find parking, turn right to reach the elevated bridge. Turn left at the T-Junction onto Saalebröcke and the road turns right across the river; there is a large parking area on the island.

Walk across the bridge onto the pedestrianised main street where the castle ruins overlook the market place. The bridges were demolished as Task Force Baum approached, forcing the column to detour north along the Sinn valley. However, when 4th Armoured Division arrived on 4 April the Germans put up a determined resistance on the west bank before withdrawing across the river. GIs crossed the following day in assault boats but the town was only cleared after a second crossing was made east of the town. Gemünden was in ruins by the time 4th Armoured Division left. Many of the buildings have been rebuilt in their original style in the post war years. Return to your car and turn left out of the entrance and retrace the route, turning right beyond the river bridge over the Main and left at the bottom of the ramp.

Turn right at the roundabout for Rieneck, and as the road climbs the hill, turn into the track on the left after 400m into the parking place, signposted for Kreigsgräbenstädt. Follow the sign for Zum Ehernfriedhof and a path leads to the German war cemetery in the woods. Soldiers killed in Gemünden were buried here after the battle along with 120 civilians killed in the fighting. There is a panoramic view across the Main valley as you look back towards the town. Return to your car and continue up the hill.

Follow the road as it drops down into the Sinn valley and through Rieneck,

Marienburg Castle has stood guard over the River Main for centuries.

following the main road as it turns right next to the church, and carry on through Burgsinn. Take the turning for Gräfendorf after the railway bridge, just beyond the village, and follow the winding road as it climbs through the forest. There are panoramic views across Gräfendorf as the road descends steeply; turn left at the T-junction for Weisenbach at the bottom of the hill. Turn right for Weickersgröben 1/2 mile beyond Gräfendorf.

The road twists and turns as it climbs out of the valley; turn left at the T-junction at the top of the hill. Again turn left at a second T-junction, signposted for Hammelburg. After 3½ miles turn right at the traffic lights for Lager Hammelburg; the camp is at the top of the hill.

The camp has changed over the past sixty years but the prison enclosures were to the right of the road. The original entrance has been blocked off but it is possible to stop for a short time in a parking area close to the new entrance a little further on. The camp is still active so it is not advisable to take photographs.

Directions to Wurzburg

Turning round at the camp entrance, retrace the route towards Hammelburg. There is a parking area on the right near the top of the hill with magnificent views across Hammelburg town and the Saale valley. Turn left at the traffic lights at the bottom of the hill, heading for Karlstadt on Route 27. The road bypasses Höllrich after 6 miles, where German troops and assault guns blocked Task Force Baum's escape route from the camp. Baum's men were trapped in the woods on Ressenburg hill, to the left. Continues straight on for 9 miles towards Karlstadt, taking in the splendid views over the town as the road descends into the Main valley.

The town had been shelled for three days before 42nd Infantry Division entered on 7 April. The river bridge had already been demolished but the American engineers had soon built a new bridge on the piers.

Turn left onto Route 27 at the T-junction, heading south for Wurzburg. The road follows the River Main along the foot of the steep hillsides and their vineyards. After 14 miles the road swings to the left as it heads into the city of Wurzburg. Away to the right is our next stop Marienburg Castle on the far bank of the river.

Keep to the right hand lane, taking the slip road signposted for Stadtmitte (town centre) and head through the underpass. Turn right at the third set of traffic lights onto Freidensbrücke (400m beyond the underpass) and cross the river. Follow Luitpoldstrasse and turn left at the second set of lights onto Wurzstrasse (250m beyond the bridge), signposted for Route 27 and Route 8. Head straight up the hill and the entrance to Feste Marienburg is to the left after ½ mile.

Follow the road through the castle moat and the archway beneath the outer wall to find parking spaces. The entrance to the castle is through a second tunnel.

Marienburg Castle is open from 9:00am to 6:00pm. It is a splendid example of German military architecture and a walk along the battlements gives a bird's eye view of the city and the surrounding countryside.

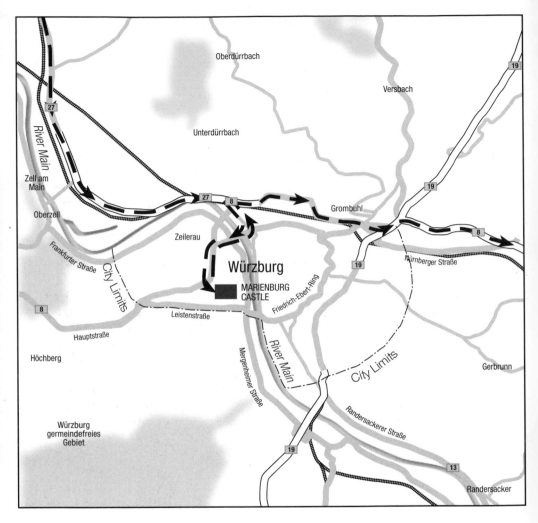

Würzburg.

Chapter Four

WURZBURG

T HERE HAVE BEEN FORTIFICATIONS on Marienburg Hill for 3,000 years and the Celts chose the location in 1,000 BC to defend the ford across the River Main. Wurzburg's importance dramatically increased in the 7th Century when the Irish Bishop Kilian and his followers were martyred on the east bank. A cathedral was consecrated on the site in 788 and fortifications were added a hundred years later to protect the inhabitants against marauding tribes. Work started on the new cathedral in 1040 and it was consecrated in 1188. A bridge, the first of three, replaced the ford in 1133.

The bishops' residence, or Palace of Palaces, is the largest building in the city and although it was started in 1720, it took twenty-five years to build. The huge U-shaped structure has dozens of huge rooms connected by large sweeping staircases and corridors. Today they are filled with exquisite furniture, pieces of art and are decorated with tapestries, paintings and frescos. The building was badly damaged during an Allied bombing raid in March 1945 but it was returned to its former glory after the war.

Even though Archduke Charles of Austria defeated French troops north of the town in 1796, the Napoleonic Wars brought the bishops' rule to an end and the town was integrated into Bavaria in 1814. The markets and traders flourished in the later part of the 19th Century but Wurzburg had to wait until the Nazis swept to power in the 1930s before it was awarded city status.

Marienburg Castle

Marienburg or Mary's Hill is named after St Mary's Church. The church was consecrated in the 8th Century and it stands next to the original forty-metre high keep in the castle courtyard. The bishops were in constant conflict with the townspeople throughout the Middle Ages and Bishop Lobdeburg moved into Marienburg Castle in 1253 for safety. The Scherenberg Gate was added in the 15th Century to protect the only route onto the cliff top and it kept the peasants at bay during the 1525 revolt. Julius Echter added Renaissance fortifications at the end of the 16th Century but they were no match for the Swedish mercenaries who captured the castle in 1631 during the Thirty Years' War.

Johann Phillip von Schönborn started major improvements when peace returned to Wurzburg, adding a new bastion and arsenal in front of the

From humble beginnings the castle has grown into a large Baroque fortress.

The original Castle Keep stands in the centre of the courtyard next to St Mary's Church.

original gate. Extra towers and gardens were also built overlooking the town. The military took over the castle and turned it into a fortress when the reigning bishop moved into the residence. The castle survived a month long siege in 1800 and Napoleon repeatedly praised it during his three visits; one of his garrisons held out for six months during the winter of 1813-14. Artillery fire set the arsenal ablaze in the Austro-Prussian War of 1866 bringing the castle's status as a fortification to an end and it was turned into a barracks soon afterwards.

Renovations in the 1930s were short lived. The buildings were reduced to rubble during an Allied bombing raid in March 1945, and 42nd Division occupied the shell when they reached the city at the beginning of April.

The castle now houses the Main-Franconian Museum, with artefacts from the surrounding area covering the past 3,000 years, including St Kilian's war banner, the oldest in Germany. A collection of Tilman Riemenschneider's 15th and 16th Century Gothic sculptures are kept in the castle in memory of a man who was tortured in the dungeons for supporting the peasants.

Air Raid over Wurzburg

By the end of 1944 German industry had been virtually destroyed and Bomber Command turned its attentions to new targets, targets that would hasten the German collapse ahead of the Allied Armies. Wing Commander Arthur Fawssett, Bomber Command's targeting officer, began to compile a list in January 1945. He chose towns that were easy to locate and the huge sweeping arc of the Main River flanked by the Marienburg Castle and the Palace of Palaces made Wurzburg a prime target. After the firestorm at Hamburg in

The ruins of Marienburg Castle after the air raid.

April 1943, where large parts of the city were destroyed by fire, it was clear that wooden housing was vulnerable to attack by incendiary bombs. Dresden was razed to the ground in a similar fashion in February 1945 and before long it was Wurzburg's turn. Although the British ministry of economic warfare had only identified one potential target, a small power station, the town's narrow streets and closely packed wooden buildings were just what RAF Bomber Command wanted.

On the night of 16 March 226 Lancaster bombers took off for Wurzburg and although the crews had been told they were attacking an important communications centre, it was obvious that their loads of incendiary bombs would start large fires in the town. As the air raid sirens screamed their warnings, the bombers dropped nearly 1,000 tons of bombs in seventeen minutes, killing hundreds and injuring thousands (almost 5,000 people lost their lives). As fires swept out of control through the old town, the people of Wurzburg watched helplessly as the flames consumed their homes. By dawn over eighty percent of the town had been destroyed, leaving 90,000 Wurzburgers homeless. A few days after the raid, Winston Churchill circulated a memorandum to his chiefs of staff:

> *The moment has come when the question of bombing of German cities simply for the sake of increasing the terror, though under other pretexts, should be reviewed.*

The bombing caused devastation amongst the wooden buildings of Wurzburg.

General Collins studied Wurzburg and the River Main from the eastern ramparts.

Otherwise we shall come into control of an utterly ruined land.

The memorandum came too late for the people of Wurzburg and two weeks later they had to face another threat, as German troops poured into their town ahead of the Seventh American Army. Once again Wurzburg's position astride the River Main meant that it was a significant military target, only this time for the men of the 42nd Rainbow Division.

The Battle for Wurzburg

While 14th Armoured Division prepared to battle its way towards Hammelburg, General Ernest Harmon, known as *Old Gravel Voice* to the GIs, ordered 42nd Division into line on XXI Corps' southern flank. On 1 April 222nd Regiment captured Wertheim astride the Main, and as the Germans withdrew, 232nd Regiment had no difficulty crossing upstream at Mark Heidenfeld. Moving quickly east, both Regiments were in a position to attack Wurzburg by the end of the following day.

The sweeping curve of the Main through the town meant that the Germans had been forced to abandon the west bank of the river and take refuge in the ruined town, destroying the three bridges as they withdrew. From the battlements of Marienburg Castle, Major-General Harry Collins could see that

GIs pick their way through the ruins looking for snipers.

222nd Regiment had to cross the Main while the Germans fired from the buildings lining the east bank. It was going to be a dangerous operation, where the bridgehead would be vulnerable to counterattacks until a large area of the town had been cleared.

As Collins and his staff contemplated what lay ahead, Colonel Henry Luongo was able to offer a glimmer of hope. One of 2nd Battalion's patrols had located a rowing boat and they had crossed the river without being seen. Seizing the chance to surprise the Germans, Collins ordered Luongo to start moving men across the river while it was dark and throughout the night the little boat went backwards and forwards across the Main, taking a handful of men at a time. As the numbers grew, the GIs quietly infiltrated buildings along the river front, waiting for their chance to strike at dawn.

At first light on 3 April the area was smoke screened and hidden GIs emerged from it to overwhelm the German outposts overlooking the river.

Assault boats carried Colonel Luongo's 2nd Battalion across the Main and by nightfall two battalions had secured a large bridgehead. Casualties had been light. While rafts and DUKWs worked around the clock ferrying tank destroyers, jeeps and supplies to the east bank, 222nd Regiment pushed deep into the town. Engineers had also been busy, building a Bailey Bridge across the damaged Alte Mainbrücke, and by the following morning 232nd Regiment had crossed.

With the help of 692nd Tank Destroyer Battalion's huge self-propelled howitzers, General Collins' men went to work clearing the city. The Germans had no formal military structure but a retired army colonel had assumed command of the units and stragglers who had reached his town. With the help of the townspeople, he had turned the ruins into a network of strongpoints. Barricades blocked every street, while the Germans used tunnels and sewers to move around the town, often reoccupying buildings after they had been cleared. Snipers, machine guns and booby traps met the GIs at every corner but it was a one sided battle and by nightfall 42nd Division had cleared hundreds of buildings. During the night German troops made a final suicidal charge towards the Bailey Bridge in 232nd Regiment's sector in the hope of cutting the American supply line. They were mown down.

The following morning 42nd Division cleared the rest of the town, and by nightfall General Collins' men had rounded up over 2,500 prisoners. As the GIs regrouped in the smoking ruins, many took the opportunity to sample the

American engineers worked around the clock to repair Alte Mainbrücke (the Old Main Bridge).

Crew of an M5 Stuart tank look on as German officers lead their men into captivity.

huge stocks of champagne that had been 'liberated'; although water was scarce, Wurzburg would always be remembered for its champagne.

As the American troops moved on to their next objective, the Wurzburgers set about restoring their city. Once the rubble had been cleared work began and the ancient stone facades formed the basis for new buildings. After twenty-five years of rebuilding Wurzburg was complete with new structures integrated with the old. Vineyards clinging to the surrounding hillsides compliment the old town's Baroque architecture and the town has a Mediterranean feel during the summer months.

Directions from Wurzburg to Furth

Retrace your route out of Wurzburg castle and turn right out of the entrance, heading down the hill. Turn right onto Luitpoldstrasse, signposted for Stadtmitte at the second set of traffic lights. Cross the River Main via Freidensbrıcke (there is a parking area just before the bridge, signposted Talavera to the left, if you wish to explore the riverbank and the town). Turn first left at the lights and carry straight on under the underpass, taking the right hand lane following the slip road for Neustadt and Kitzingen. Follow signs for Route 8 out of Wurzburg, signposted for Kitzingen and Nuremberg.

Keep straight on through Kitzingen and turn right for Ipbofen at the roundabout at the far side of the town. The road bypasses the walled village of Mainbernhein; take the third exit for Ipbofen at the roundabout at the far side of the village. Continue straight on for 22 miles to Neustadt. Immediately after crossing the Aisch stream, turn left at the traffic lights and bypass the town (as the Americans did); take the second exit for Nırnberg at the roundabout beyond the town.

Chapter Five

THE ROAD TO NUREMBERG

HAVING DEALT WITH WURZBURG and the neighbouring town of Schweinfurt, General Wade Haislip was given the task of capturing Nuremberg, the most German of German cities. 3rd Division and 45th Division were closing in from the north while 42nd Division had just finished clearing Wurzburg to the northwest. General Patch had ordered Major-General Harry Collins to join XV Corps and engage troops holding the town of Furth to the west of Nuremberg. The plan was for the 42nd and 45th to cut the Munich autobahn to the south, while 3rd Division cleared the outskirts north of the River Pegnitz. As soon as all three divisions were in position the battle for the city centre would begin, a task that no one relished.

During the early hours of 15 April, GIs from 30th Regiment easily crossed the Pegnitz in 3rd Division's area, fifteen miles north of Nuremberg. Lieutenant-Colonel Christopher Chaney's 3rd Battalion then crossed the Ludwig Canal around Baiersdorf. The rest of the division followed, moving into the woods northeast of Erlangen and by nightfall Major-General John O'Daniel was ready to leave in moving towards the city.

The engineers worked around the clock to build new bridges for General Collins' tanks.

45th Division had further to travel and two regiments crossed the Wiesant River as soon as it was light and headed south. 157th Regiment moved quickly to the north bank of the Pegnitz over twenty miles away and 1st Battalion had established a bridgehead at Lauf by nightfall. 179th Regiment also moved fast from Kirchenrenbach and it overtook several columns of German soldiers heading towards the city. The speed of the American advance had taken many by surprise and resistance was non-existent in many villages, only the *Luftwaffe* seemed to be organised.

On 16 April 42nd Rainbow Division joined the advance, heading southeast from Wurzburg with two infantry regiments mounted on anything that had an engine. After passing through Kitzingen and Iphofen the 42nd Reconnaissance Troop found a strong rearguard covering the bridges along the River Aisch in Neustadt. General Collins quickly revised the march routes and 222nd Regiment crossed north of the town, while 232nd slipped over the river to the south. 242nd Regiment made sure the Germans did not escape. By nightfall Neustadt had been surrounded and 42nd Division was ready to resume the advance (the garrison surrendered as soon as they realised they had been outflanked).

The Encirclement of Nuremberg

3rd Division began to move towards Nuremberg on 16 April and as soon as 7th Regiment had cleared Erlangen, the German colonel surrendered the town before committing suicide. Meanwhile, 15th Regiment battled against 88mm

flak guns and infantry in the woods around Kalchreuth and Buchenbuhl as it moved towards the River Pegnitz. 1st Battalion also found self-propelled guns in Heroldsberg and called up its own tanks and tank destroyers to corner them. In some villages the local *Volkssturm* had been forced to fight by SS troops and many had chosen to get drunk before their final battle. The main danger was the dozens of 20mm anti-aircraft guns covering the roads, positioned to slow the American advance towards Nuremberg and they allowed the main German units to withdraw into the city to make their last stand. One by one the villages of

A local Volkssturm member receives instruction in the use of the deadly Panzerfaust.

Having cleared Wurzburg, 42nd Rainbow Division faced a long drive to Nuremberg.

Kraftshof, Kleinreuth and Thon fell as 3rd Division moved closer to the Pegnitz.

45th Division continued to advance east of the city and in 157th Regiment's sector, 2nd Battalion covered the Lauf bridgehead while two armoured columns supported 1st Battalion's advance. By midday they had secured a large autobahn intersection, allowing 2nd Battalion to move into Röthenbach. While the armour moved along the autobahn towards Fischbach, the infantry fanned out into the thick forests, hunting for snipers who had been left behind to harass the advance. Artillery rounds crashed through the trees as Colonel O'Brien's men edged forward and many of the shells were fired by two batteries of 88s dug in near the Regiment's objective. By nightfall the batteries had been overrun and as 3rd Battalion moved into line, the whole Regiment wheeled through the Reichswald getting across the Munich autobahn.

On the division's northern flank, 179th Regiment kept the bulk of its force north of the River Pegnitz and pushed through the Reichswald towards the northeast corner of the city, making contact with 3rd Division. For the first time the American troops discovered what the Germans had in store for them, and it was a terrifying prospect. Nuremberg was ringed by dozens of 88mm anti-aircraft guns. Although they had been placed to protect the city during bombing raids, the versatile weapons were able to fire both armour piercing and high-explosive rounds at ground targets. *Volkssturm* units and civilians had spent the past few days building roadblocks to protect the gun batteries while infantry units and tanks poured into Nuremberg from every direction. The German plan was to fight to the last for the city.

180th Regiment moved up into the centre of 45th Division's front and after clearing Fischbach it came under small arms and flak fire from Langerwasser where tens of thousands of men and women had once camped during the Nuremberg Rallies. The woods were cleared by midnight, leaving Lieutenant-Colonel Everett Duvall wondering what was waiting for his men on the Rally Grounds; would there be a last symbolic stand by Nazi fanatics or would they have fled into the heart of the city?

XV Corps had taken hundreds of prisoners during the day but one women taken by 45th Division attracted the attention of the intelligence officers: Mrs Fritz Kuhn, wife of the German-American Bund leader. The movement had

Having come under small arms fire, this tank has reduced a building to a flaming inferno.

A youthful anti-aircraft 88 gun crew form a defence line with the gun positioned in the ground defence role.

been founded in America in 1935 but Kuhn's rallies in New York's Madison Square had stirred up American resentment towards Germany, angering Hitler. The Bund was disowned by the German Nazi Party and it folded when America entered the war at the end of 1941.

By 17 April XV Corps' grip on Nuremberg was tightening. 3rd and 45th Divisions were engaged in the outskirts of the city, all that was left was for 42nd Division to seal off the western approaches. The German plan had been to fight a rearguard action in Furth but Collins' successful move around Neustadt meant that his men reached Furth a day earlier than expected. While 232nd Regiment swung to the south of Furth the rest of the division closed in on the town and by nightfall it had been surrounded.

There was no spectacular advance in 3rd Division's sector. General O'Daniel's men were facing a seemingly impenetrable barrier of flak batteries, however, the 88 guns had one weakness – they were immobile. Careful reconnaissance, both on the ground and in the air, pinpointed many of the guns, and the American artillery pounded the German positions while the infantry and armour moved into position. Smoke smothered the batteries as the GIs made their final assault. The advance was slow but one-by-one 3rd

Division overran the German defences and by nightfall over fifty 88s had been captured.

15th Regiment was the first to enter the ruins in the afternoon and Lieutenant Frank Burke, 1st Battalion's transportation officer was in the thick of the fighting. After going forward to select a suitable parking area for his supply vehicles, Burke came across a group of about ten Germans preparing to counter-attack. Running back to the nearest company, he snatched a submachine gun and returned to engage the enemy soldiers. The group returned fire with their submachine guns, rifles, and *panzerfausts* but the American officer scattered them, killing the crew of a hidden machine gun as he ran. Having run out of ammunition, Burke grabbed a discarded rifle and ran one hundred yards down the street through heavy fire, diving behind a disabled tank to engage a second German squad. When a sniper opened fire from a nearby cellar, the officer ran to the window and fired a full clip at the sniper before diving in to kill him. After withdrawing to find a new rifle and grenades, Burke returned to his one-man crusade but failed to hit anything with the rifle. Undeterred, he pulled the pins from two grenades and ran into the enemy-held building, throwing them as a German grenade landed at his feet. It was suicidal. The three explosions in the confined room killed the Germans but Burke staggered out covered in dust and grabbed his rifle. After killing four more Germans, one of them as he charged forward firing his submachine gun from the hip, Burke withdrew. He remained at the front for some time, leading two platoons as they fought off infantry and tank attacks.

In four hours of action, Burke had single-handedly killed eleven and wounded another three enemy soldiers before playing a leading role in the battalion's advance; he was awarded the Medal of Honour for his actions.

South and east of the city, 45th Division was heavily engaged in the suburbs of the city throughout the afternoon. Small arms, machine gun, mortar, 88 and 20mm flak gunfire rattled through the streets as twelve battalions of American artillery pounded the buildings and fighter-bombers swooped low overhead.

On the division's right flank, 179th Regiment advanced over a mile along the south bank of the Pegnitz River. After driving off a strong counter-attack by infantry and self-propelled guns, two companies penetrated the ring of anti-aircraft guns while the rest of Lieutenant-Colonel William Grace's men struggled to cross Regensburg railway. The Germans had positioned flak guns and strongpoints to cover every underpass.

There was heavy fighting in the centre, where 180th Regiment inched slowly towards the Nazi Rally Grounds in the face of withering fire. The highlight of the day was the liberation of 13,000 Allied prisoners of war by 2nd Battalion; many were Russian but the GIs found 250 American and 450 British prisoners amongst the crowds.

157th Regiment was busy extending the division's left flank, looking to close the gap with 42nd Division, and in doing so it captured a large number

Barricades could only delay the inevitable result in Furth.

XV Corps was soon cutting across country to form a strong cordon around Nuremberg.

of 20mm and 88mm gun emplacements. By nightfall 45th Division had made deep penetrations into Nuremberg's southeast suburbs, capturing over 4,800 prisoners and neutralising forty-five 88s.

The Battle for Furth

To the west of Nuremberg, the citizens of Furth had spent the past few days building strongpoints and roadblocks as soldiers poured into the town. They had large amounts of small arms and ammunition but they had no armour and had lost radio contact with the artillery batteries around Nuremberg. By sidestepping Neustadt, 42nd Division had encircled Furth a day earlier than expected, taking the Germans by surprise and the plan to make a fighting withdrawal into Nuremberg no longer applied; General Collins' men had already encircled the town.

Two battalions of 222nd Regiment attacked from the west at dawn on 18 April as the remaining battalion moved in from the north. Fighting was fierce, but the American artillery and armour gave the GIs all the advantages, and the cordon slowly tightened as the hours passed. The battle raged throughout the night but by daybreak on the 19th it was over and white flags hung from every building. The townspeople were put to work clearing the streets removing roadblocks as 8,000 prisoners were marched into captivity; men who could have bolstered the dwindling Nuremberg garrison.

The capture of Furth allowed 42nd Division to link up with 45th Division south of Nuremberg. With all roads cut, the men trapped inside the American cordon prepared to fight to the last; the battle for the city was about to begin in earnest.

German prisoners taken in the fighting for Furth.

German prisoners throwing down their rifles.

Directions to the Nuremberg (Nürnberg) Rally Grounds

Continue along route 8 (it becomes a dual carriageway after 10 minutes) and bypass Furth. The road becomes Autobahn 73 after another 17 miles. Exit at junction 34 for Zollhaus and Nürnberg, turn left at the top of the slip road signposted for Zentrum and head north along Route 8 for 3 miles. After bypassing Messa Stadium to the right, turn right into Bayernstrasse, signposted for Dokumentationszentrum. The Congress Hall is immediately ahead. Turn right into the car park to visit the Document Centre and the Rally Grounds.

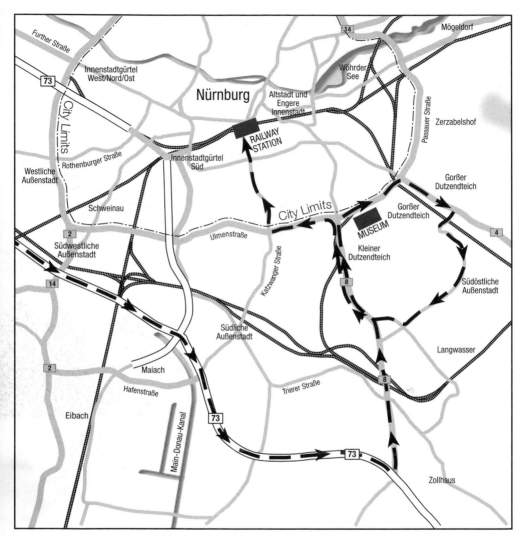

Road to the Nürnberg Rally Grounds.

Chapter Six

NUREMBERG

NUREMBERG SITS ASTRIDE THE RIVER PEGNITZ and it is the second largest city in Bavaria with 500,000 inhabitants. It was first mentioned in 1050 and the fertile Franconian Plains ensured success for its growing markets. The Emperors of the Holy Roman Empire built an Imperial Castle on a rocky outcrop overlooking the centre of the walled city, and their royal courts (known as Diets) were held here from 1356. The Imperial insignia was brought to the city in 1426 and it remained in the city for over 350 years.

Nuremberg Castle stands guard over the heart of the old city.

The city walls were completed around 1400 and the moat was finished fifty years later, encompassing both the city and the castle. Continuing feuds, known as the Markgraves' Wars, between the Emperor's representative in Nuremberg and the Imperial troops troubled the city for the next two centuries while plagues decimated the population. Nuremberg remained neutral during the Thirty Years' War and the Treaty of Nuremberg brought hostilities to an end but thousands had died from disease during the conflict. The city was eventually annexed to Bavaria in 1806 following Napoleon's defeat of the Prussians.

Nuremberg Rally Grounds

The Dutzendteich area, two miles south east of Nuremberg's old town, had been an area where people could relax in the parks, walk round the lakes or visit the zoo and the sports arenas. In 1927, Franconia's Gauleiter, Julius Streicher suggested using the area to stage a Party Rally. It was the first of many Nazi rallies in the city and over the years that followed the area became the focal point for the annual *Reichsparteitage* (Reich Party Rally). Year after year new structures were added as the Rally Grounds expanded they eventually covered eleven square kilometres.

The initial improvement works were small, as the Nazis converted existing structures for their own use, but Albert Speer was commissioned to redesign

A poster calling Party members to the 1934 rally, the Rally of Will.

the *Parteitagsgelände* (Party Rally Grounds) in 1934. The huge project included adding conference halls, parade grounds and exhibition centres while the meticulous programme anticipated that the work would not be complete until August 1945. Using huge amounts of labour, (slave labour at places such as the Mauthausen granite quarries) work progressed at a rapid rate but the 1939 Rally was cancelled when Germany invaded Poland. Interest in the Rally Grounds then declined, and work ground to a halt as the tide of war turned in the Allies' favour.

45th Division captured the area on 18 April 1945 and a few days later the first of many ceremonies were held to celebrate the liberation of the city. It was known as the Soldiers' Field during the American occupation and jazz bands and baseball games were held where the Nazi organisations had once paraded in front of their Führer.

Dutzendteich is once again an area of leisure but many of the Nazi structures are still standing in various states of decay. It is possible to walk and drive around the Rally Grounds but it is advisable to start a tour with a visit to the *Dokumentationszentrum* in the Congress Hall where films and photographs illustrate what happened here in the 1930s.

The Nazi Rallies

The *Reichsparteitage* was the highlight of the Nazi Party calendar and it grew from humble beginnings into a week long festival of processions, rallies, speeches and wargames. The first Rally was held in Munich in 1923, followed by a second three years later in Weimar. As the Nazi Party grew in size, the leaders realised that the large gatherings were a perfect opportunity for members to hear their views and for the world to see how their numbers were growing.

Julius Streicher suggested Nuremberg with its excellent rail connections, well organised local party and a sympathetic police force. The Rally became a bi-annual event, starting in 1927, and an annual event called the *Reichsparteitage des deutschen Volkes* held every September after the Nazis seized power in 1933 and each rally was given a theme relating to current events:

Hitler's rousing speeches were the central feature of every Rally.

1933   *Reichsparteitag des Sieges* – Rally of Victory

        The seizure of power and the victory over the Weimar Republic.

1934   Initially the rally did not have a theme. Alternate titles were later attributed to it:

        Reichsparteitag der Einheit und Stärke – Rally of Unity and Strength

        Reichsparteitag der Macht – Rally of Power

        Reichsparteitag des Willens – Rally of Will (from Leni Riefenstahl's movie)

1935   *Reichsparteitag der Freiheit* – Rally of Freedom

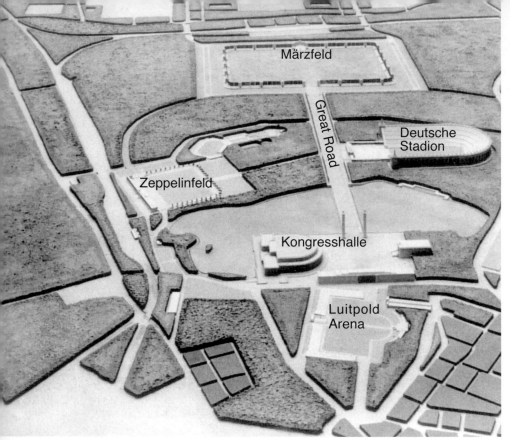

Albert Speer's architectural model for the completed grounds; work was abandoned when war broke out and many buildings were never finished.

The liberation from the Treaty of Versailles by the introduction of conscription. Herman Göring announced the Nuremberg Laws during the Rally, legalising the separation of Jews from society and paving the way for the Holocaust.

1936 *Reichsparteitag der Ehre* – Rally of Honour

The restoration of honour by the occupation of the Rhineland.

1937 *Reichsparteitag der Arbeit* – Rally of Labour

The reduction of unemployment under the Nazis.

1938 *Reichsparteitag Großdeutschland* – Rally of Greater Germany

Celebrating the annexation of Austria. The Imperial insignia was returned to the town during the Rally.

The 1939 Rally was cancelled following Germany's invasion of Poland on 1 September; ironically it would have been titled *Reichsparteitag des Friedens*, the Rally of Peace.

The Kongresshalle which houses the Dokumentationszentrum (Documentation Centre), a museum dedicated to the history of the Nuremberg Rally Grounds and the part they played in the rise of the Nazi Party.

In the days before the Rally, thousands of members would travel across Germany to Nuremberg, assembling on one of the many camping grounds around the city. Each organisation, the SS, SA, Hitler Youth etc, had its own area and while some stayed in temporary buildings, others lived under canvas.

The main focus of the Rally was on Adolf Hitler and day after day men and women gathered in one of the arenas to listen to his speeches or one made by the other Party leaders. Each day showcased a different organisation of the Party, the State or one of the Armed Forces. The *Wehrmacht*, the German Labour Front, the Hitler Youth and League of German Girls were just a few of the organisations that put on displays.

Albert Speer displays plans for an early rally at the Luitpold area.

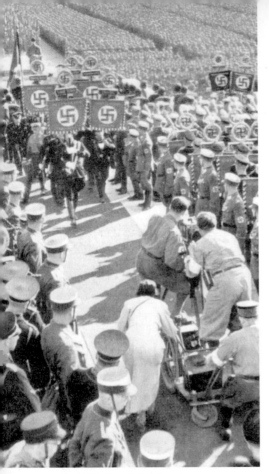

Parades were an important part of the rallies and each organisation took its turn to march in front of the Führer. Many parades were held in the city, and hour after hour processions marched through the flag draped streets of the old town to the Hauptmarkt (renamed Adolf-Hitler-Platz in 1933) where the Führer stood, arm outstretched in the Nazi salute, by the Schöner Brunnen (the Beautiful Fountain).

Richard Wagner was Hitler's favourite composer and between 1935 and 1938 the Rally was opened with a presentation of the *Meistersinger*, an opera expressing Germany's world view.

The Nazi press published various yearbooks, some with illustrations and others with transcripts of the speeches, as a memento of the Rally. The Nazi Party newspaper, the *Völkischer Beobachter*, also printed special Rally editions.

The German filmmaker, Leni Riefenstahl, produced a documentary film of the 1933 Rally entitled *Sieg des Glaubens*, however, few people saw it. Shortly after the film appeared, Ernst

Leni Riefenstahl directs a camera crew during the filming of Triumph of the Will.

Both military and civilian Nazi organisations took turns to entertain the crowds. Here the Young Girls' Movement put on a display.

Röhm, leader of the SA, was murdered during the Night of the Long Knives, a purge of so-called traitors in the Nazi Party, and his image was banned. A second film, *Triumph of the Will* (Triumph des Willens) was made in 1934 and it has passed into film history for its portrayal of the hypnotic and overwhelming spectacle of the Nuremberg Rally.

TOURING THE GROUNDS

Documentation Centre

A museum dedicated to the history of the Nuremberg Rally Grounds and the part they played in the rise of the Nazi Party is located in the north wing of the Congress Hall. There is a car park (a small fee is charged) by the side of the Congress Hall and the museum is entered via a covered flight of steps jutting out from the northwest corner of the building.

Address   Faszination und Gewalt (Fascination and Terror)
           Dokumentationszentrum Reichsparteitagsgelände
           Bayernstraße 110
           90471 Nürnberg

  Tel: (0911) 231-5666   Fax: (0911) 231-8410
E-Mail: dokumentationszentrum@stadt.nuernberg.de

The museum is open from 9:00am until 6:00pm on weekdays and from 10:00am until 6:00pm on weekends. The admission fees in 2005 were five Euros for adults, 2.5 Euros for children, with special reduced rates for large parties and school groups. The exhibits are in German but English (and other) language handsets are available.

The upper level has a permanent exhibition and the visitor is guided through nineteen chronologically arranged areas, covering the rise and fall of the National Socialist movement and the part played by the Nuremberg Party Rally Grounds. The final part of the visit gives access to a walkway projecting into the heart of the Congress Hall and visitors can compare the crumbling brick walls with the outer granite façade. There are a number of temporary exhibits on display on the lower floor as well as a café and bookshop.

Kongreßhalle (Congress Hall)

Work started on the building in 1935 and it was intended to replace the smaller *Luitpoldhalle*, having space for 50,000 people to be seated undercover. Franz and Ludwig Ruff planned their building along the lines of the Coliseum in Rome and a full-scale model of part of the building showed visitors what to expect. Work was abandoned in 1943 before the interior seating area and the roof had been completed and the structure has been left incomplete. It now houses the Document Centre, the Nuremberg Symphony Orchestra and storage areas.

Two huge obelisks were supposed to stand astride the Great Road alongside the Hall and the area to the west was going to be a permanent exhibition centre. They never got past the design stage and the area is now used as a car park and for Nuremberg's biannual fairground. The area beyond the car park was the Nuremberg Zoo and it was closed by the Nazis to make way for a new Culture Hall; again the building never got beyond the drawing board.

Directions to Luitpold Arena

Cross the main road, Bayernstrasse, immediately outside the Congress Hall and enter Luitpoldhain Park (or Luitpold Grove).

The area had staged the Bavarian State Trade Exhibition since 1906 and the park and hall were the venues for the first two Rallies in 1927 and 1929. In 1930 a First World War Memorial, or Ehrenhalle (Hall of Honour), was erected in the park but it was soon taken over as a focal point for the Nazi Parades. The Ehrenhalle is a useful orientation point; it is found on the east side of the park.

The Municipal Administration Department made early improvements to turn the area into a parade ground and stands were added between 1933 and 1937 under Albert Speer's direction, increasing the capacity to 150,000. A large grandstand, complete with a speaker's platform and three tall swastika banners, stood opposite the Hall of Honour. A large wooden eagle later framed the platform and permanent structures were added as the years passed.

As well as parades and speeches, the arena was the scene for a ceremony honouring the war dead. As the silent ranks of soldiers flanked the granite avenue, Hitler and his leaders marched from the podium across the arena to the Ehrenhalle, where they saluted the *Blutfahne* (the Blood Flag from the 1923 Munich putsch) and laid a memorial wreath. It was just one of many symbolic ceremonies that typified the Nuremberg rallies.

The grandstands were removed after the war and the area reverted to being a park. The Ehrenhalle has reverted to its originally purpose as War Memorial and a dedication to the victims of the Nazi regime has been added.

Luitpoldhalle

The exhibition hall stood at the southwest corner of Luitpold Arena. It was built for the 1906 State Trade Exhibition and between 1933 and 1935 Albert Speer redesigned the building for Party Congresses. Senior party members gathered in the buildings to hear speeches by their leaders. The building was badly damaged during the Allied air raids and the ruins were removed after the war, only the steps remain.

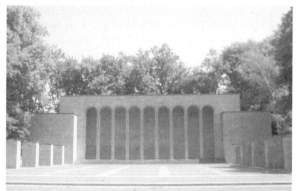

Above left: The architects drew their inspiration from Roman amphitheatres.

Above: The incomplete interior exposes the brick walls.

Left: The war memorial in Luitpold Arena was taken over by the Nazi Party and turned into a focal point for ceremonies. It is now dedicated to the victims of the Nazis.

Below: Rudolph Hess and Albert Speer accompany Hitler during a visit to the Luitpold Arena; the shaven-headed Julius Streicher is on the right.

Awaiting the crowds, hundreds of swastikas flutter in the breeze by the Luitpoldhalle.

Mass swastikas paraded through the Luitpold arena.

The Yankee Doodlers play jazz music for GIs who are seated where Hitler once spoke to the masses.

The Great Road today stretches into the distance.

Großestraße (The Great Road)

Re-cross Bayernstrasse either by the footbridge (signposted Kurt Klutentreter Steg) or at street level to visit the Great Road.

The Great Road passes between the Dutzendteich Lakes, twin lakes that were once surrounded by parks and beer gardens. At eighty metres wide and over two kilometres long the Road is an impressive piece of architecture built for the cancelled 1939 Rally. The road was designed to connect Luitpold Arena to

The Zeppelintribüne evolved into a huge grandstand.

Flags once adorned the towers surrounding the Zeppelin Field.

The Cathedral of Light was an unforgettable spectacle.

the Mars Field, forming a central axis for the grounds. Albert Speer designed the road to align with Nuremberg's Castle, symbolically linking the Nazi Rally Grounds with the city's Imperial heritage. Many of the original slabs at the north end have been restored and sections of the ruined steps built for the crowds can be seen along the east edge. The Great Road served as a landing strip for the American Air Force immediately after the city was captured; it is now used as an overflow parking area for the Trade Fair Centre.

Great Deutsche Stadion (The Great German Stadium)

Albert Speer planned to build a large stone podium halfway down the east side of the Great Road for Hitler to take the salute of the passing parades but his greatest project would have stood immediately opposite. The Great

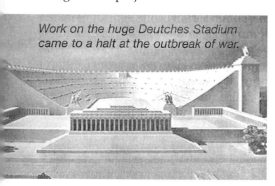

Work on the huge Deutches Stadium came to a halt at the outbreak of war.

German Stadium was going to be the largest stadium in the world and the horseshoe shaped structure would have held 400,000 (it would have been three times larger than one of the ancient Egyptian pyramids). Although the foundation stone was dedicated on 9 September 1937 only a small part of the excavations had been carried out by the time work was abandoned in 1942.

The stone was removed in 2001 and Silbersee, a lake formed by the excavations and Silberbuck, a hill made of rubble from the bombed city, now occupy the site. Nürnberger Messe, the Nuremberg Trade Fair Centre, home of the annual Toy Fair, is just to the south.

Directions to the Zeppelinfeld

Return to your car and turn right on leaving the museum car park. After 700 metres turn right at the traffic lights just beyond the railway underpass; head south and turn right at a second set of lights in 700 metres. Note the Transformer Building (Umspannwerk) to the right just before the crossroads. The large building was built to supply the electricity needed to power the searchlights used during the night time parades on Zeppelinfeld. The derelict building has hardly changed and the chipped out eagle and swastika over the doorway can still be seen.

Head under the railway bridge and follow the road as it turns right and then left. The Zeppelinfeld is immediately in front. Park your car to visit the Zeppelintribüne.

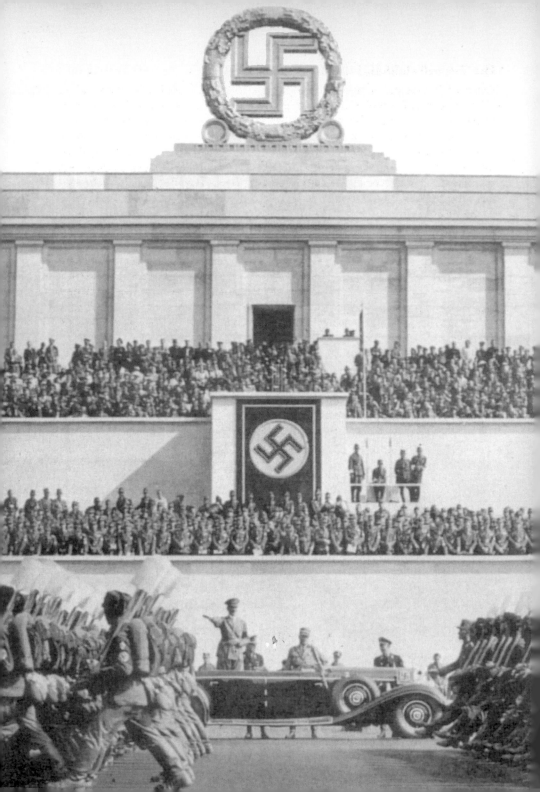

The Zeppelinfeld and the Zeppelintribüne

Zeppelinfeld was an open-air stadium first used for parades in 1934 before Albert Speer had completed his final plan for the parade ground. The enclosed arena had a large grandstand, called the *Zeppelintribüne*, on its east side and the large wooden eagle above the speaker's podium was soon replaced by a huge gilt swastika. The *Zeppelinfeld* was finished by 1936 and, while thirty-four columns surrounded the field and a Hall of Pillars (*Pfeilerhalle*), flanked the grandstand. The arena was decked with flags during the day and lit up by 120 searchlights at night; the columns of light created a fantastic spectacle known as the *Lichtdom* (Cathedral of Light). Huge cauldrons filled with burning oil surrounded the entire *Zeppelintribüne* with flames, completing the display. The gathered masses waited in anticipation, erupting in cries of *Heil Hitler* and *Sieg Heil* as the doors of the *Zeppelintribüne* opened and Hitler emerged to take his place on the speaker's podium. Speer had designed the spectacle with maximum impact and sense of belonging to the Party.

Left: Hitler takes the salute at the foot of the Zeppelintribüne.

Below: The same view today; only the steps and the central building still remain.

On 22 April 1945 3rd Division paraded on the *Zeppelinfeld* as General Alexander Patch awarded five Medals of Honour to members of the division. A large Stars and Stripes was hung over the swastika on top of the grandstand and three days later explosives blew it to pieces.

A closer study of the crumbling remains of the *Zeppelintribüne* reveals that the structure was only built from brick and then faced with marble to give the impression of a solid imposing structure. The Hall of Pillars was demolished in 1967 after they became unstable and the upper parts of the structure were removed a few years later. It is possible to climb the decaying steps and stand on Hitler's podium where steps and a higher railing have been added. The arena is now used for leisure activities and concerts; part of the Nuremberg city racetrack passes immediately in front of the *Zeppelintribüne*.

Otto Schweizer redesigned the original Municipal Stadium, south of the *Zeppelinfeld*, between 1933 and 1937 and it was used to stage the Day of the

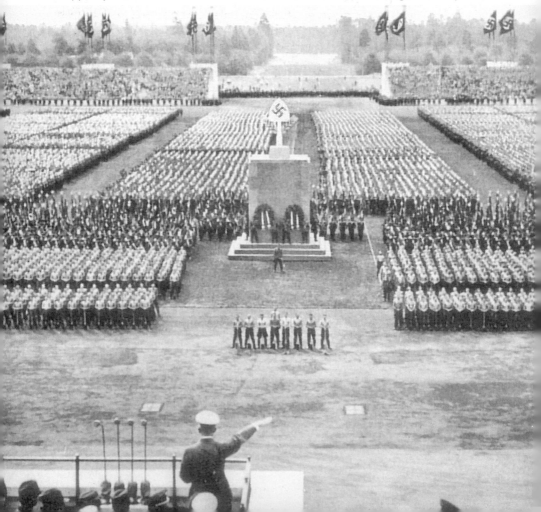

Hitler Youth. Thousands of children staged athletics displays before the Nazi leaders before listening to political speeches. A new stadium was started in 1937 but it was not completed until 1942 and never used. The modern Municipal Stadium, called the *Frankenstadion*, has a swimming pool, allotments and a campsite.

Directions to the Märzfeld (the March Field)

Return to your car and head southeast (with the Zeppelintribüne immediately behind you) along Beuthhenerstrasse. The road curves to the right and becomes Schönlebenstrasse as it crosses the Great Road to the right after 1 mile. The site of Märzfeld (March Field) was to the left of the road.

Albert Speer intended to build a large open structure at the south end of the Great Road to replace the *Zeppelinfeld*. It would have been 600 metres along its longest side with twenty-six towers topped with sculptures by Josef Thorak and a huge statue of the goddess of victory taller than the Statue of Liberty overlooking the arena. There would have been seating for 160,000 spectators so they could watch huge parades and Army war games. Only eleven towers had been completed when work stopped in 1943 and they were demolished by 1967 to make way for the tower blocks of Langwasser suburb. Large parts of the area have been built over and only a few crumbling remains of foundations can still be found hiding in the bushes.

Left: Hitler gives the salute from the speakers' podium at the Zeppelinfeld.

Below: The same view today.

The Camping Grounds

Huge camping grounds were built across southern Nuremberg, each dedicated to one of the Nazi Organisations. The largest camp, Langerwasser, to the south of *Märzfeld*, could accommodate 200,000 men. All that remains today is a water tower standing on a hill overlooking the old camping grounds. A new railway station was built for the visitors between *Märzfeld* and the camps; only the ruins are left.

Directions to Nuremberg Railway Station (Bahnhof)

Continue past the Great Road and turn right at the traffic lights, heading north along Münchenerstrasse towards the centre of Nuremberg. Turn left at the first set of traffic lights and then right at the next traffic lights into Altersbergerstrasse.

The large building on the left was the SS barracks,

One of the huge camps surrounding the Rally Grounds.

Below: Hitler inspects the guard of honour outside the Town Hall.

built between 1936 and 1939; they were used as a training facility for radio operators during the war. The complex was the headquarters for the 2nd US Armoured Cavalry Regiment and known as the Merrell Barracks after the war. Only the front of the original building remains and the new building was returned to the German government in 1995.

Heading north, the road heads under a railway tunnel after 1 mile; the railway station is 200 to the west of the tunnel. Take note of the location and park your vehicle in one of the many on street parking places in the area. Walk back to the station to start your visit of Nuremberg's old town.

A Walking Tour of Nuremberg (see map on page 136)

Hitler made a triumphant entrance at the Hauptbahnhof at the start of the Rallies and thousands gathered around the station in the hope of glimpsing the Führer while the SS guards kept them at bay. The city centre was decked with flags during the rallies and the Nazi organisations paraded through the streets to the main market place by day and by night as the crowds looked on.

Across the road from the railway station is Königstor, one of the many medieval towers protecting the city wall; follow Königstrasse, to the right of the tower, heading into the centre of the city. Thousands of onlookers lined the streets to watch the endless parades as swastika flags fluttered from every window. The streets are still full, but shoppers now crowd the shops, cafés and markets. Continue past St Lawrence's Church (St Lorenzer's) on the right and cross Pegnitz River on Museumsbrücke. The Hauptmarkt is 100m beyond the river.

The square has served as a market place since the 14th Century and it is the focal point of the famous annual Christmas Market. The 14th Century Church of Our Lady (*Frauenkirche*) is on the east side while the new town hall (*Rathaus*) stands at the northwest corner; the original building was destroyed during the war. The focal point of the square is the multi-tiered ornate *Schöner Brunnen* (the Beautiful Fountain) rising sixty feet into the air in front of the town hall.

Adolf Hitler stood by the fountain, surrounded by his henchmen and they reviewed the passing columns of troops as they marched along the west side

Hitler salutes his troops as they march past during the 1934 Rally. Leni Riefenstahl can be seen directing a movie camera beneath his raised arm.

Present-day photograph showing the route taken by the parades. The troops passed the Town Hall and marched up the hill towards the castle.

of the square heading up the hill towards the castle.

Hauptmarkt was renamed Adolf-Hitler-Platz in 1933 but the Americans called it Eiserner-Michael-Platz, or Iron Mike Square, in honour of 3rd Division's General, John O'Daniel. Troops held a parade in the square on the evening of 20 April 1945 (Hitler's birthday) after the three-day battle for the city.

Continuing up Burgstrasse enter Nuremberg Castle via the Heaven's Gate at the top of the hill.

Nuremberg Castle opening hours:
9:00am to 17:00pm April to September
10:00am to 16:00pm October to March.

Emperor Heinrich III built the original Imperial Castle, or *Kaiserberg* on an outcrop of rock overlooking the city. A new wall was built in the 11th Century to protect the rulers of the Holy Roman Empire while they held their Imperial Deits and trials inside. A guardian, or castellan, was soon appointed to look after the Empire's concerns and one built the adjacent Burgrave's Castle. There was constant friction between the Burgrave and the Emperor and Imperial troops were forced to occupy both castles in 1389. The Burgrave's castle was eventually returned to its owner but it burnt down in 1420 following further disagreements; it was sold to the Emperor a few years later. Two attempts to recapture it failed.

Right: Nazis mingle with the crowds on Museum Bridge; Fleisch Bridge is in the background.

Below: Fleisch Bridge today.

There are impressive views across the old city walls and towers from the top of the Sinwell Tower and the huge Emperor's Hall, Knight's Hall and Imperial Stables are just some of the buildings that are now home to various museums.

After visiting the castle, retrace your steps back to Hauptmarkt and continue straight on, leaving the square at the southwest corner and cross the river via Fleischbrücke.

112

Streicher's offices.

Turn left after 100m onto Kaiserstrasse and then right onto Königstrasse. Turn left onto Lorenzerstrasse alongside St Lorenzer's Church, heading east. Continue straight on along Marienstrasse after passing beneath Mareintor Gate, another of the gates in the city wall. The Gauhaus stands on the north side (left hand side) of Marienplatz.

The building was erected in 1937 for the Franconia Gauleiter (Nazi Party area administrator), Julius Streicher. It was severely damaged during the battle for the city but it was rebuilt in the original 1930s style after the war. Streicher accompanied Hitler during the 1923 Munich Putsch and he was rewarded with the Gauleiter post two years later. He was violently anti-semitic and used his weekly newspaper *Der Stürmer*, to voice his opinions and rouse racial hatred. Streicher's mixture of corruption, sadism and greed made him unpopular and he was dismissed from his post in 1940. He was found guilty of stirring racial hatred during the Nuremberg Trials and was executed.

Anti-Semitic newspaper, Der Stürmer.

Julius Streicher, Franconia's vicious Gauleiter and number one Jew baiter.

Head back along Marienstrasse and take the first left into Gleissbihlstrasse; the railway station is at the end of the street.

Opposite the station is the Grand Hotel and it was a centre of entertainment for the American delegation during the period of the Nuremberg trials. The building had suffered bomb damage but emergency repairs allowed engineers to install a café, a restaurant, relaxation rooms and a dance hall. The Russian staff had strict instructions to keep their distance as the international relations between the Allies soured.

Deutscher Hof Hotel, where Hitler stayed during the Rallies, is 400m to the west. He occupied a large first floor room and often reviewed troops from the window as they marched past. The building was extended in 1936 and the

Hitler stayed at the Deutscher Hof Hotel during the Rallies.

The streets would be full of expectant crowds as flags hung from the buildings during the Rallies; they are now full of shoppers searching the markets for a bargain. St Lorenzer's Church is in the background.

The Führer watches a torchlight procession from his balcony.

Führer's new room had a balcony. This side of the hotel has been remodelled and the balcony no longer exists, but the original part of the building has not been changed.

Directions to the Nuremberg Courtrooms

Head west (either walking or driving) from the hotel along Frauentorgraben. Continue straight on along Am Plarner, where the city walls run north; it becomes Sudliche Further Strasse after a short distance. The Nuremberg

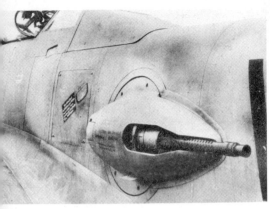

Me 410's remote controlled barbette which could be swivelled to point upwards to fire into the fuel tanks of Allied bombers.

Halifax Mk III bomber.
German 88s defending the Reich from the RAF.

Nightfighter Me 410. Its upward firing cannon is being examined.

Palace of Justice is to the right after 3/4 mile.

During the Second World War two important events took place in Nuremberg. The Royal Air Force had its heaviest losses over the city during a disastrous bombing raid in March 1944. Twelve months later American troops closed in on the ruins during the advance across Southern Germany.

The Nuremberg Raid

With the declaration of war, Nuremberg became an important industrial centre with its factories producing armaments and munitions for the German armed forces. As the tide turned against the *Luftwaffe* and the Allied Air Forces flew deeper raids across Germany, Nuremberg found itself on the Royal Air Force's target list and on the evening of 31 March 1944, 782 bombers left airfields across England heading for the city. Early forecasts had reported that the skies over Germany were clear and there was little chance of cloud except over the city, where the aircrew needed it the least. Despite the reports, Bomber Command decided to press ahead, placing their faith in the 7,000 plus officers and men flying the Halifaxs, Lancasters and Mosquitoes.

The raid started badly, and over

fifty planes turned back with technical problems before they crossed the Belgian coast, but the rest pressed on. The weather proved to be changeable as high winds pushed many planes off course or behind schedule and conflicting reports sent by the Pathfinders only confused the picture as the bombers flew over Liege towards the German border.

Although diversionary flights had been directed across Europe, the *Luftwaffe* had guessed where the main raid was heading and fighter squadrons across Germany scrambled and headed into the skies; over 200 Ju 88s, Me 109s, FW 190s and Me 110 night fighters were being vectored towards the bomber stream.

Thirteen planes fell victim to the anti-aircraft guns lining what was known as Flak Alley along the River Rhine. The clear, moonlit sky silhouetted the bombers and conspicuous vapour trails, normally only seen at higher operating heights, had started to form, making them easy to target. Many of the night fighters were equipped with the new twin 20mm cannons, code-named *Schröage Musik*. The guns pointed upwards, allowing the pilots to fly beneath the bombers, into their blind spots, and target their fuel tanks. While *Oberleutnant* Martin Becker shot down six, *Oberleutnant* Helmut Schulte and *Leutnant* Wilhelm Seuss claimed four each. All together sixty-nine planes were shot down between the Rhine and Nuremberg.

One plane damaged during the air battle was the Halifax 'Excalibur' with 578 Squadron. The navigator, bomb aimer and wireless operator had baled out following a confusing radio message but Pilot Officer Cyril Barton decided to press on to the target.

As the ragged formations made their final approach it was obvious that the target was covered with low cloud as the high winds blew many pilots off course. The Pathfinders were supposed to drop flares and showers of radar interrupting Window (bundles of thin strips of aluminium that showered the sky) over Nuremberg but some crews dropped their loads ten miles northeast of the target. The second wave of Pathfinders were equally confused and there was a long line of burning target markers along the horizon by the time the bombers reached the target. One Mosquito dropped its flares over Schweinfurt due to faulty equipment and around fifty crews dropped their bombs on the town's ball-bearing factories. This part of the raid could be considered a success but the town was over forty miles from Nuremberg! Another thirteen bombers became totally lost and their pilots headed for home after jettisoning their loads.

The rest struggled on through a wall of flak as the pilots steadied their aircraft for the final approach and the bomb aimers tried to make sense of the scattered flares below. The

Pilot Officer Cyril Joe Barton VC.

Window had been scattered far and wide, leaving the flak guns free to engage the bombers and they claimed thirty-nine over the target area. The bombs killed 133 civilians and another 11,000 were left homeless but damage to Nuremberg's industry was minimal; only three large factories had been seriously damaged.

As they turned for home the remaining crews were met by a strong headwind, halving their speed as they, once again, flew through the waves of night fighters roaming the skies. Another dozen planes were shot down, two crashed in mid air and fourteen crashed in England having run out of fuel. Pilot Officer Barton had managed to bomb the target and nurse his crippled Halifax back across the Channel before it ran out of fuel. The twenty-two-year-old pilot crashed his plane into the yards of Ryhope Colliery, County Durham, after clipping the last dwelling in a row of miners' houses. Flying debris killed one miner and injured another. Three of the crew survived the crash, unfortunately Cyril Barton died of his injuries thirty minutes later. He was posthumously awarded the Victoria Cross.

Bomber Command lost 104 planes on what became known as Black Friday, ninety-four of them to enemy action; only ten German fighters had been shot down; 745 airmen had been killed or injured and another 159 had been taken prisoner. When he was interviewed by Alastair Revie, the author of the book *The Lost Command*, Sir Arthur 'Bomber' Harris summed up his feelings about

Rear fuselage of Cyril Barton's Halifax where it came to rest in Ryhope Colliery yard.

Air raids and severe fighting virtually destroyed Nuremberg.

the officers and men under his command:

> *They knew the odds were constantly against them to the point that they were playing never-ending games of Russian Roulette. I do not know why or how they went on as they did. I am lost in admiration for them.*

The Royal Air Force returned with a vengeance on the night of 2 January 1945. This time the Pathfinders were greeted with clear skies over the city and accurately marked their targets ahead of 514 Lancaster bombers. Hundreds of tonnes of high explosive and incendiary bombs wreaked havoc across large parts of Nuremberg, in particular in the old town; the castle, many of the churches and over 2,000 timber medieval houses were burnt to the ground in the inferno that followed. Bomber Command's targets, the MAN factory, the Siemens factory and the railway sidings were devastated; altogether over 400 industrial buildings had been destroyed. Some would say it was the perfect bombing raid but many bombs fell on surrounding suburbs; 1,800 civilians

were killed and another 100,000 had been left homeless.

Over the next twenty years architects and builders worked together to restore the old town to its former glory and a walk along the streets reveals ancient buildings, churches and busy markets. Nuremberg has certainly risen from the ashes after a chequered history.

The Battle for Nuremberg

In April 1945 3rd Division and 45th Division faced three *Kampfgruppen* in Nuremberg and while the first was built around 1st Battalion, *38th SS-Panzergrenadier Regiment*, the rest of the SS troops joined *Kampfgruppe Dirnagel*. Air force personnel and officer cadets based in the city had been formed into *Kampfgruppe Rienow* and both the local police force and firemen had also armed themselves and taken up positions in the ruins. They would be helped by thousands of civilians who had stayed behind to fight for their city, either with weapons or by building barricades and carrying supplies. Yet again it was going to be a fight to the last man.

The battle for the city began in earnest on 18 April and in 3rd Division's sector, 7th Regiment crossed the airport to the north, only to find a line of anti-aircraft guns waiting for them. Private Joseph Merrell started a private crusade after his platoon was pinned down in Lohe. He began by running 100 yards through a hail of bullets to shoot four Germans at point blank range. Although a sniper's bullet smashed his rifle, he continued forward another 200 yards under fire, hurling two grenades into a machine-gun nest, before

120

grabbing a pistol to finish off the crew. He was seriously wounded as he crept forward but still staggered forwards to toss a grenade into a second emplacement; the brave GI was killed as he fell onto the stunned crew. Private Merrell had killed twenty-three Germans and opened the way for 3rd Battalion's advance; he was posthumously awarded the Medal of Honour. 2nd Battalion took over the lead and headed into the St Johannis district where snipers appeared to be watching from every window.

From now on the infantry relied on their armour and artillery to blast apart buildings as they edged forward and 15th Regiment systematically reduced

GIs shelter behind a tank while the crew reduces a strongpoint to rubble in a previously undamged part of the city.

The infantry and tanks had to work closely together in the ruined city.

The ruins provided perfect cover for machine gun nests and snipers.

many buildings to rubble as it battled its way through the northeast corner of the city. 2nd Battalion relentlessly shelled four apartment blocks in the Schopperhof district until they were burning out of control and then stood back to watch the fires. 3rd Battalion also came under heavy fire in the Klein district and had to withdraw until the artillery had demolished the buildings. Casualties were high, but 3rd Division kept up the pressure, edging forward from house to house, and city block to city block.

To the southeast, 45th Division continued to push towards the heart of the city, and although most of the German artillery had been overrun the day before, the rattle of machine gun and sniper fire and the crack of anti-tank and guns increased by the hour. The desperate measures that some Nazis would go to were illustrated during the afternoon when a Storch observation plane crashed in 179th Regiment's area. The light observation plane was not designed to carry armament but the pilot had secured six *panzerfausts* to its wings and rigged up firing devices to the cockpit. He was shot down before he attempted to carry out his suicidal plan. 180th Regiment inched forward against stiff resistance but the tanks and artillery silenced machine gun posts one by one and the fighting died down as the Germans withdrew into the heart of the city.

The GIs marvelled at the bold décor of the Luitpold arena and the Zeppelinfield as they moved cautiously across the Rally Grounds. Artillery and mortar rounds deafened the soldiers rather than, as in the past, shouts of 'Heil Hitler'. GIs went on to discover dozens of German soldiers huddled beneath the concrete stands. American public relations officers had planned to hoist the Stars and Stripes over Luitpold Stadium on 20 April (a birthday present for Hitler), but 45th Division hoisted its own flag a couple of days early. On the division's south flank, 157th Regiment faced fierce resistance as it fought its way to Ludwig Canal, seizing bridges across the waterway by

Laufer Tower fell when tank destroyers arrived and threatened to raze the structure to the ground.

Street by street and block by block, the Americans closed in on the old city but progress was extremely slow.

nightfall.

Throughout 19 April XV Corps closed in as the German commanders pulled their troops back into the heart of the city, leaving rearguards and snipers to cover the withdrawal. The ancient moat covering the thick medieval walls would stop the American tanks and give protection from the artillery and mortar shells raining down on the ruins. 15th Regiment's 1st Battalion pushed deep into the suburbs and captured 140 members of the Nuremberg police holding the buildings surrounding the Westfriedhof cemetery. One company was soon across the River Pegnitz and Colonel Edson's men were closing in on the city walls by nightfall. After clearing St Johannis Hospital, 7th Regiment advanced towards the city walls from the north but as Colonel Heintges' men prepared for its final assault *Luftwaffe* trainees emerged from Nuremberg's Castle in a suicidal attack. They were cut to pieces.

Lieutenant Michael Daly went forward alone when the twisted wreckage of a railway bridge stopped his company on Bayreutherstrasse. Sergeant Roy Kurtz later recalled what happened:

Lieutenant Daly had just begun to climb up a low embankment along the railroad when a machine gun suddenly opened up on us from the other side of Leipziger Platz. We were caught out in the open by rapid traversing fire and our men were killed left and right. Realising that the whole company was threatened with annihilation, the lieutenant ran toward the machine gun, a conspicuous target as he crossed the tracks, to some rubble within fifty yards of the enemy gun. He killed all the German gunners with his carbine and pushed on forward, ahead of his company, until he sighted an enemy anti-tank detachment which was zeroed in on our attached armour units.

Sergeant Ivan Ketron's account continues the story:

He was taking his life in his hands and we all knew it. I saw the Lieutenant work his way forward to what was left of a house and open fire with his carbine. The Krauts replied with a rain of automatic fire that sent up eddies of fine white dust from the building he was shooting from. Then panzerfaust rockets began to slam against the furthest wall of the building. Although the whole Kraut patrol was concentrating on him, Lieutenant Daly kept firing his carbine until he killed six Germans and silenced the enemy fire. Leading his men forward once more, he entered a public park, well ahead of his troops. As he paused to place his platoons in position, two Germans rushed forward from concealment and set up a machine gun only ten yards from the Lieutenant. An American sergeant fell dead at the first burst and Lieutenant Daly seized the M-1 that was lying on the ground and took up a pointblank fire fight which resulted in the killing of the enemy MG crew.

Lieutenant Daly continued in a similar fashion throughout the fighting for Nuremberg, always acting as the company scout, risking his life to protect his men on many occasions. He was awarded the Medal of Honour, 3rd Division's third in as many days.

In 30th Regiment's sector a fierce attack led by the city's Gauleiter threatened to overrun one of 2nd Battalion's companies but Captain Robert Fleet's men refused to withdraw and battled with the Germans until they retired. As 2nd Battalion regrouped, 1st Battalion led the advance along the north bank of the Pegnitz River and by noon it had reached the northeast corner of the walled town. Lieutenant Tremblay's anti-tank platoon kept the Germans holding Laufer Tower (one of the turrets on the medieval wall) trapped inside until bazooka teams and tank destroyers moved into position. A white flag soon appeared and 125 prisoners emerged, opening the way into the walled city.

The story was the same in the southern part of Nuremberg, where resistance increased as 45th Division pushed the Germans back towards the city walls. In 157th Regiment's sector it was late afternoon before one of 1st Battalion's companies broke into the industrial district south of the SS Barracks and Colonel O'Brien pushed the rest of the battalion through the narrow gap while the *SS Kampfgruppe* withdrew towards the railway station. 3rd Battalion worked its way though the MAN Industrial Plant but 2nd Battalion found its way forward blocked. One company had to keep the Germans under fire as the rest of the battalion probed a small weak spot and pushed deep into the suburbs on a narrow front. After cutting the Furth road, it turned northwest to

XV Corps 'liberated' a ruined city, laid to waste by air raids and ground fighting.

General Iron Mike O'Daniel salutes his 'Dog-faced Soldiers'.

link up with 3rd Division on the River Pegnitz; a risky strategy designed to stop the Germans making another stand. General Frederick's plan worked and by nightfall all three of 157th Regiment's battalions were lodged deep in Nuremberg's suburbs. 180th Regiment was also closing in on the city walls, capturing hundreds of prisoners as it fought past machine guns, snipers and anti-tank guns along the roads to Königstor.

The final assault was made on 20 April and although the German soldiers were cornered, outgunned and low on ammunition, they were determined to hold out to the end. One by one the GIs cleared the ruined buildings, pulling their enemies out of basements, tunnels and air raid shelters. By midday, 3rd Division reached Adolf Hitler Platz but the final group of two hundred soldiers continued to fight well into the night; they eventually died to a man after explosives were lowered into their tunnel. Nuremberg 'the most German of German cities' had been cleared and 45th Division alone had rounded up 2,637 prisoners, bringing its total to around 10,000; it was estimated that another 1,500 Germans had been killed or wounded.

As the afternoon sky began to darken, a rifle platoon from each of 3rd Division's regiments lined up alongside tanks and tank destroyers as the Stars and Stripes was raised above Adolf Hitler Platz and the band played the American National Anthem. It was Hitler's birthday and 3rd Division's 'gift' was to rename it Eiserner Michael Platz, or Iron Mike Square, after their divisional commander. General O'Daniel gave the following speech to the tired GIs:

Again the 3rd Division has taken its objective. We are standing at the site of the stronghold of Nazi resistance in our zone. Through your feats of arms, you have smashed fifty heavy anti-aircraft guns, captured four thousand prisoners, and driven the Hun from every house and every castle and bunker in our part of Nuremberg. I congratulate you upon your superior performance.

The band followed with the division's theme tune, the 'Dog-faced Soldier':

> I wouldn't give a bean, to be a fancy pants Marine,
> I'd rather be a dog-faced soldier like I am.
> I wouldn't trade my old ODs, for all the Navy's dungarees,
> For I'm the walking pride of Uncle Sam.
> On all the posters that I read it says the Army builds men,
> So they're tearing me down to build me over again.
> I'm just a dog-faced soldier with a rifle on my shoulder,
> And I eat a Kraut for breakfast every day.
> So feed me ammunition, keep me in the 3rd Division,
> Your dog-faced soldier boy's okay!

XV Corps held its formal flag-raising ceremony in Eiserner Michael Platz the following day as the weary GIs marched to their assembly areas.

Badly damaged buildings surround the courtrooms; the prison stands in the semi-circular compound.

Courtroom 600

The Nuremberg Trials

The decision to try to punish those responsible for war crimes had been made at the Moscow conferences as early as 1943, while further discussions between the Allied leaders at Teheran, Jalta and Potsdam laid the foundations for an International Military Tribunal. In the final days of the war the Moscow Declaration made it clear that the Allies intended to bring to justice the men and women who were responsible for perpetrating massacres and atrocities across Nazi occupied Europe. Hundred of thousands of men, women and children had been enslaved, starved, maltreated, tortured and murdered because of their political or religious beliefs. The terms 'wars of aggression', 'genocide' and 'war crimes' are well known today, but they were a new legal concept in 1945; the Nazis had perpetrated crimes against humanity on a scale that had never been witnessed before.

The Moscow Declaration was confirmed on 8 August 1945 with the formation of an International Military Tribunal composed of members from the United States, the Soviet Union, Great Britain and France, and their objective was clear: they were to bring the senior Nazi officials to trial. The International Military Tribunal opened on 18 October 1945, in Berlin's Supreme Court Building and they agreed to hold the first trial in the American Zone where facilities had been prepared in Nuremberg. (Future international military tribunals were planned but they were cancelled due to the deteriorating relationships between the Soviet Union and the rest of the Allies.)

Courtroom 600 is behind the large windows on the top floor.

The Nuremberg Trials began in November 1945 and in the following month the International Military Tribunal declared a new law defining four categories of 'war crimes' and 'crimes against peace and humanity':

1. Conspiracy to commit crimes against peace
2. Planning, initiating and waging wars of aggression
3. War crimes
4. Crimes against humanity

The defendants faced different combinations of the four categories, according to their roles in the Nazi hierarchy, but in each case the prosecution had no legal precedence to compare the case against. (The extermination of the Jews, in particular, was a new experience in modern history, and the Holocaust had not been defined as a separate crime for that reason.)

The term Nuremberg Trials includes the International Military Trial of twenty-four Nazi leaders between November 1945 and August 1946 and eleven other trials between December 1946 and July 1948 brought against the military, administrative, diplomatic, legal, industrial and medical organisations that were either run by the Nazis or profited from their regime.

Nuremberg was chosen because it had one of the only buildings large enough to hold the trials left standing in Germany. The German Museum in Munich was the Americans' first choice but General Patton had already turned the building into an officers' club and he refused to relocate. The Palace of Justice was one of the few buildings still standing in the ruins of Nuremberg, and in July eighty American engineers and 500 German workers began work repairing the bomb damage and making alterations ready for the International Military Trials.

Over the next five months the west wing of the Palace of Justice was turned into offices for 2,500 staff with a PX (military shop) and refectory in the basement. Further offices and a large press room occupied the east wing where the room that would be the focus for the world's attention for eight months was situated; Courtroom 600.

The question of security was paramount and the star-shaped prison within the grounds and its three floors were large enough to accommodate all the prisoners. A tunnel led into the courthouse and a lift brought the prisoners directly into the courtroom reducing the security risk to a minimum.

Before the start of the trials, Robert Ley, the head of the Nazi Labour Front, committed suicide, resulting in changes to the prisoners' accommodation. The light fittings were modified and lightweight tables were introduced to stop the men hanging themselves; wire netting was also erected along the wings to stop anyone jumping off the balconies. A close watch was kept on the prisoners to stop them taking poison while armed guards and tanks covered every entrance to stop unauthorised visitors or attacks on the building.

Courtroom 600

The courtroom is only open on Saturdays and Sundays, between 2:00pm and 4:00pm, and tours are held every 30 minutes. The guided tour takes you straight to the courtroom where photographs and film footage are used to describe what happened in the famous room. The rest of the complex has hardly changed and still functions as Nuremberg's court. The prison block where the Nazi leaders were held was to the rear of the building but it was demolished in recent years; the gymnasium where the guilty were hanged has also disappeared

Courtroom 600 was returned to its original state when the trials were over, however, many features are still visible. The windows were blacked out during the trial for security purposes and modern fluorescent lights and spotlights

Guards surround the twenty-one defendants.

replaced the original lighting to satisfy the film and camera crews recording the trial. The press and other spectators sat on rows of chairs just inside the entrance, while a balcony (removed after the trial) increased the seating to 250. The press secretaries sat to the right, in front of the press, alongside the four prosecution attorneys, one from each country:

Sir Hartley Shawcross of Great Britain

Robert Jackson from the USA

Roman Rudenko from the USSR

Chief Prosecutor Champetier de Ribes from France

The eight judges sat along the right hand wall on a low platform beneath the windows; there were two representatives from each country:

France: Robert Falco and Henri Donnedieu de Vabres

USA: John Parker and Francis Biddle

Great Britain: Chief Judge Lord Justice Geoffrey Lawrence

    and Norman Birkett

USSR: Iona Nikitchenko and Alexander Volchkov

The lectern for the attorneys stood to the right, in front of the prosecution team. Court secretaries and stenographers sat in front of the judges and the witnesses stood at the far end. Graphic documentary films, depicting the Nazi atrocities, were projected onto a huge film screen filling the far wall. The court bailiff and twelve translators sat in the far left corner. IBM had designed equipment capable of simultaneously translating transcripts into or from four languages. It was harrowing work for the young interpreters as they concentrated on translating the horrific accounts. They had control over proceedings by illuminating a yellow light bulb if they could not keep up or a red bulb if they had lost track of the transcript. The translations were immediately transmitted on 300 headsets distributed around the courtroom while loudspeakers relayed the proceedings to the adjacent pressroom. On busy days the room was overflowing with the reporters, authors, ministers, senators, diplomats, historians and generals; very few Germans attended.

Right: The judges sat in front of the blacked out windows.

Below: Many of the original features were restored after the trials.

Below right: Herman Göring stands and addresses the court; to his left are Rudolf Hess, Joachim von Ribbentrop and Wilhelm Keitel.

The twenty-one defendants sat on two rows of seats along the left hand wall. The list of defendants is given from left to right:

Front row

Hermann Göring	Mobilised the Reich's economic resources for rearmament
Rudolf Hess	The Führer's deputy until he flew to Scotland in May 1941
Joachim von Ribbentrop	Foreign Minister from 1938 to 1945
Wilhelm Keitel	Army *Feldmarschall*
Ernst Kaltenbrunner	Head of the Security Police (SD)
Alfred Rosenberg	Minister for the Eastern occupied territories after 1941
Hans Frank	Governor-General of Poland after 1939
Wilhelm Frick	Minister for Internal Affairs
Julius Streicher	Anti-Semitic publisher and Franconia's Gauleiter until 1940
Walter Funk	Minister for Economic Affairs and President of the Central Bank
Horace Schacht	President of the Reichsbank and Minister of Economics

Rear row

Karl Dönitz	Admiral of the German Fleet and Hitler's successor
Erich Raeder	Commander-in-Chief of the Navy from 1943
Baldur von Schirach	Head of the Hitler Youth and Gauleiter of Vienna after 1940
Fritz Sauckel	Head of the concentration camp system after 1942
Alfred Jodl	Head of *OKW* and Hitler's advisor on strategy and operations
Franz von Papen	Hitler's first vice-chancellor then ambassador in Vienna and Ankara
Arthur Seyss-Inquart	Commissioner for the Netherlands during the occupation
Albert Speer	Minister for Weapons and Munitions after 1942
Konstantin von Neurath	Protector of Bohemia and Moravia between 1939 and 1943

| Hans Fritzsche | Head of the news service section in the Ministry for Propaganda |

Not present

Adolf Hitler	Führer and leader of the NSDAP (committed suicide in Berlin)
Martin Bormann	Chief of the party chancellery (presumed dead)
Heinrich Himmler	Chief of the Gestapo and other senior posts (committed suicide after his capture by Allied troops)
Robert Ley	Head of the Labour Front from 1933 (committed suicide in Nuremberg)
Gustav von Krupp	Head of the armaments company (too ill to appear)

The Allies paid for sixteen defence attorneys and over one hundred staff to represent the Nazi leaders; they were seated in front of the accused.

Although uniforms (without badges of rank) were available, the majority wore simple suits and they were guarded by American military police dressed in immaculate uniforms, complete with white helmets, belts and batons. The assembled group looked like a group of businessmen rather than the perpetrators of crimes against humanity and genocide.

While Albert Speer tried to distance himself from the rest of the accused, a slimmed down Hermann Göring proved to be the star defendant, often outwitting the prosecuting team; he was eventually separated from the group. Over 4,000 tons of paperwork had been seized and brought to Nuremberg where hundreds of staff spent thousands of hours sorting and translating the mountain of documents. Over 300,000 affidavits and statements presented overwhelming evidence and 236 men and women were called to give their statements in person. Total denial was the defence's main argument but it failed to impress the judges and after 218 days the verdicts were announced to the world.

Bormann

Bormann	Guilty; sentenced in absentia to death
Göring	Guilty; sentenced to death
Hess	Guilty; sentenced to life imprisonment
Ribbentrop	Guilty; sentenced to death
Keitel	Guilty; sentenced to death
Kaltenbrunner	Guilty; sentenced to death
Rosenberg	Guilty; sentenced to death
Frank	Guilty; sentenced to death

Göring

Ribbentrop   *Kaltenbrunner*   *Keitel*   *Rosenberg*   *Frank*

Frick   *Streicher*   *Sauckel*   *Jodl*   *Seyss-Inquart*

Frick	Guilty; sentenced to death
Streicher	Guilty; sentenced to death
Funk	Guilty; sentenced to life imprisonment (released in 1957 due to ill health)
Schacht	Acquitted; German officials kept him in prison until 1948
Dönitz	Guilty; 10 years' imprisonment; released in 1956
Raeder	Guilty; sentenced to life imprisonment (released in 1955 due to ill health)
Von Schirach	Guilty; sentenced to life imprisonment and released in 1966
Sauckel	Guilty; sentenced to death
Jodl	Guilty; sentenced to death
Von Papen	Acquitted; imprisoned for 8 years in denazification process; released 1949
Seyss-Inquart	Guilty; sentenced to death
Speer	Guilty; sentenced to life imprisonment; released in 1966
Von Neurath	Guilty; 15 years' imprisonment (released in 1954 due to ill health)
Fritzsche	Guilty; 9 years' imprisonment; released in 1950

Charges against Gustav von Krupp were dropped and he died in 1950; his son was sentenced to 12 years' imprisonment and forfeited his private property.

The executions were timed for the morning of 16 October 1946 but hours before the men were led out, Göring committed suicide, cheating the hangman. One after another the senior Nazi officials were hung in the prison's gymnasium (the building was demolished in 1987) and their bodies cremated, the ashes were strewn in the Isar River. The prisoners were taken to Berlin-Spandau jail where Hess was the final prisoner, he committed suicide in 1987.

Between December 1946 and July 1948 another eleven cases relating to Nazi War crimes were heard at Nuremberg:

Case 1   The Doctors (or Medical) Case
          Twenty-three doctors were charged with experimenting on prisoners. Sixteen were convicted; seven were sentenced to death.

Case 2   The Milch Case
          Feldmarschall Erhard Milch was convicted of murdering and torturing prisoners of war as well as carrying out high altitude and freezing experiments; sentenced to life imprisonment.

Case 3   The Justice (or Judges) Case
          Sixteen members of the Reich Ministry of Justice and the People's and Special Courts were charged with using their authority to commit war crimes or crimes against humanity. Ten were convicted and four acquitted. One member's case was declared a mistrial while the remaining defendant died in custody.

Case 4   The WVHA Case (Economic and Administrative Office)
          Oswald Pohl and seventeen members of the WVHA were charged with war crimes against prisoners held in concentration camps; three were sentenced to death, twelve were imprisoned.

Case 5   The Flick Case
          Six industrial leaders were charged with using slave labour and plundering private property; three (including Friedrich Flick) were convicted and sentenced to prison.

Case 6   The IG Farben Case
          Twenty-four members of the IG Farben industrial company were charged with war crimes (including operating the works associated with the Auschwitz extermination camp); thirteen were found guilty and given prison sentences.

Case 7   The Hostage Case
          Twelve German officers were charged with acts of devastation and murdering both surrendering troops and civilians. Eight defendants were imprisoned and two committed suicide.

Case 8   The RUSHA Case
          Himmler's Race and Settlement Office and the Office for the Strengthening of Germandom were responsible for the murder,

deportation, and torture of political opponents and members of religious and racial groups. All but one of the fourteen accused were found guilty.

Case 9　The Einsatzgruppen Case
Twenty-four members of the Einsatzgruppen (mobile execution units deployed on the Eastern Front) were charged with the murder and torture of prisoners and civilians. All were found guilty. Fourteen were sentenced to hang but ten had their sentences reduced to imprisonment.

Case 10　The Krupp Case
Twelve members of the Krupp Industrial Organisation, including Alfred Krupp, were charged with employment of slave labour and seizing property. All but one was sentenced to jail.

Case 11　The Ministries Case
Twenty-one senior members of the Nazi Party hierarchy were charged with waging war, violating international treaties and committing war crimes; nineteen were imprisoned.

The increasing tensions between the Allies brought an end to the trials and many Nazi war criminals slipped into obscurity as the denazification process continued across Germany. Nazi hunters continue to search for the senior perpetrators across the world in the hope of bringing them to justice.

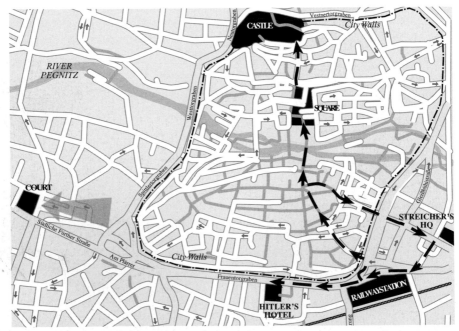

Nuremberg City centre.

Chapter Seven

CROSSING THE DANUBE

AFTER CLEARING FURTH, 42nd Division had assembled south of Nuremberg before resuming the advance south. It set off for the Danube on 21 April and over the next four days covered over fifty miles on foot, finding rearguards, snipers and mines covering every road. By nightfall on the 24th the men were exhausted, having had little sleep but there would be no let up until they had reached the Danube. By 25 April they were within striking distance of Donauworth, a small town straddling the river,

These men of 12th Armoured Division would have no doubt translated the village name Krautostheim into 'Home of the Krauts' during their advance to the Danube.

where hundreds of SS troops had gathered to defend the bridges. 20th Division had just reached XV Corps area and General Wade had sent three companies of the 27th Tank Battalion and two platoons of the 692nd Tank Destroyer Battalion forward in order to strengthen 42nd Division.

Directions from Nuremberg to Donauworth

Head under the tunnel to the west of the Railway station and turn immediate left at the far end; turn right into Alters-bergerstrasse, signposted for Munich and the autobahn, after 400m. Head south for three miles through the suburbs, turning left at the traffic lights in front of the SS Barracks. Turn right for Autobahn 6 at the first set of traffic lights and head south along Route 8 past the Rally Grounds.

Many of the towns and villages across Bavaria have changed little and the men of 45th Thunderbird Division would still recognise the gateway into Ellingen.

Join Autobahn 73, signposted for Munich but at the first junction (Junction 58) join Autobahn 6, heading southwest for Schwabach. Again leave at the first junction (Junction 57) and head south on Route 2 for Roth. The road bypasses Roth, Ellingen and Weissenberg (it is possible to go through the centre of the walled villages to follow the original route taken by the American troops) and after 35 miles it enters the Altmühl valley.

45th Division encountered only sporadic resistance as it headed south from Nuremberg but it was briefly delayed around Tretchtlingen after German engineers blew the bridges across the Altmühl stream. The advance resumed after their engineers had bridged the stream but resistance increased as General Frederick's men closed in on Donauworth and the Danube.

Continue south on Route 2, bypassing Monheim and Kaiserheim, and after 17 miles the road winds down a steep hill into Donauworth. Follow the main street as it winds through the town towards the river.

The Battle for Donauworth

Lieutenant-Colonel Donald Downard split his Task Force into two columns and they headed off at first light on 26 April, aiming to catch the Germans by surprise. Downard led a company of the 242nd Infantry mounted on tanks east towards the Danube, to cut off the escape route along the riverbank. Meanwhile, two companies of the 222nd Infantry led the second column down the main road towards Donauworth. The tanks had to bypass road blocks and three lost tracks to mines in the first five minutes (Lieutenant William Grimes, son of General Grimes, the chief of the US Army's Cavalry School was killed by one explosion). Many Germans ran at the sight of the approaching tanks and dozens were mown down, but the rest stayed at their posts to engage them with *Panzerfausts*. Company D's light tanks ran the gauntlet of fire and took two hundred prisoners in Kasheim.

The two columns entered during the late afternoon as the German engineers detonated explosives on the last remaining bridge earlier than expected, leaving many soldiers trapped in the town. With nowhere to run, they fought on until nightfall; only seventeen were captured alive, the rest fought to the death.

Donauworth stands at the confluence of the Danube and the Wörnitz.

Directions from Donauworth to Dillingen

At the bottom of the hill the road follows the river; turn right across the bridge, signposted for Dillingen and head west alongside the river. Turn left at the roundabout, heading under the railway bridge for Route 16 and Dillingen. Continue straight on at a second roundabout after 1/2 mile and head west along the Danube Valley; Dillingen is 11 miles away. The river runs parallel to the road, to the left, but trees hide it from view.

Turn left at the traffic lights into the town and again left at a second set of lights in the centre; the bridge is a short distance out of the town. Cross over the new concrete structure and turn right into the side road just beyond the river. It is possible to park and take a closer look at the river and the bridge.

The Capture of Dillingen Bridge

The town of Remagen and the Ludendorff Railway Bridge were made famous on 7 March 1945 when armoured infantry and tanks of the 9th Armoured Division used it to cross the Rhine. On that occasion mistakes made by the German High Command and local officers were compounded by problems with the explosives, leaving the bridge damaged but passable. At Dillingen, a small town twenty miles west of Donauworth, the 12th Armoured Division briefly made a bridge across the River Danube famous on 22 April for similar reasons.

The modern Dillingen bridge across the Danube.

Major-General Roderick Allen's men had been on the move since the end of March, taking part in the battles for Wurzburg, Schweinfurt and Neustadt near Nuremberg. Heading south with the tanks and halftracks advancing in a series of armoured Task Forces, the *Hellcats* had swept everything in their path aside on the road to the Danube. On the night of 21 April Brigadier-General Riley Ennis had Combat Command A deployed in two Task Forces and at 07:00 hours the two columns set off for the Danube to the south.

Task Force One managed to cover the forty miles between Dinkelsbuhl and Lauingen in good time, only to find the river bridge in ruins. Task Force Two, with a company of Shermans, a platoon of M5 Stuart light tanks from 43rd Tank Battalion and two companies of GIs from the 66th Armoured Infantry Battalion mounted in halftracks, advanced along a parallel road heading for Dillingen. Lieutenant-Colonel Clayton Wells was spurred on by intelligence reports that a camp holding 500 American prisoners was beyond the bridge. Although there was little chance of reaching the bridge before the Germans destroyed it, Wells was determined to get there as fast as possible.

It was still early when Lieutenant Charles Ippolito's light tank platoon drove into the town square, finding hundreds of soldiers milling around while a mechanised column withdrew towards the river. The Germans had not expected the Americans to arrive until later that afternoon and they had been taken completely by surprise. With guns blazing Ippolito's men drove straight through the crowds heading for the river as the rest of Task Force Two caused mayhem in the town. At the bridge several hundred metres to the south, the engineers responsible for demolishing the bridge were cut down by machine gun fire as they ran for the plunger hoping to blow up the bridge. Other Germans near the bridge were quickly rounded up while the tanks began engaging targets on the far bank.

Captain William Riddell Jr, 43rd Tank Battalion's Company commander was first onto the bridge and Sergeants J Houston and Robert Welch jumped down from the leading halftrack to follow. With bullets flying over their heads, the three men ran to the far side, shooting two Germans on the bridge, becoming the first Americans to cross the Danube. As Riddell and the others ran, Private Robert Strothers, one of Lieutenant Ippolito's crewmen was guarding a German engineer at gunpoint as he cut the wires to six 500lb bombs wired to the bridge. They would have provided the necessary explosion to set off hundreds of pounds of dynamite fixed to the bridge piers.

As more Sherman and Stuart tanks rolled up to the bridge and gave covering fire, Sergeant Lester Porter of Company A led his squad across to join the officers on the far side of the river. While the small group of GIs waited, fearful for their lives, engineers of the 199th Armoured Engineers made the bridge safe, cutting dozens of wires and throwing explosive charges into the swirling water below. They later hung a net across the river to stop the Germans floating mines downstream.

Before long Task Force Two had formed a solid bridgehead on the south bank, and waited for the counter-attacks to begin. However, the Germans were not aware that the bridge had fallen for some time and vehicles, bringing reinforcements forward to defend the riverbank, were easy targets for Captain Riddell's tank crews. Task Force Hall and Task Force Fields had soon crossed and pushed south, driving German observers from high ground overlooking Dillingen bridge.

The rest of 12th Armoured crossed the river and held the bridgehead until the 3rd Infantry Division could take it over. Although there was little chance of reaching the bridge by counter-attacks, the German artillery shelled the immediate area around the clock while *Luftwaffe* pilots made dozens of flights over the Danube, hoping to score a hit on the structure. 12th Armoured Division's mobile anti-aircraft battalion, armed with 20mm quad guns mounted on halftracks, shot down six planes in one day.

The capture of Dilligen Bridge did not hit the headlines like Remagen but it did disrupt the German plans to defend the Danube as they redeployed to contain 12th Armoured Division's bridgehead.

Directions from Dillingen to Marxheim on the River Danube

Retrace your steps into Dillingen, turning right in the square, and a second right onto Route 16, heading northeast through Höchstädt and Tapfheim towards Donauworth. Take the slip road onto the roundabout on the outskirts of Donauworth and continue straight on into the town, passing beneath a railway bridge. Turn immediate right at the roundabout, and carry straight on at two sets of traffic lights, following the River Womitz. The road turns sharp left across the river and then to

Lorries carry treadway units down to the river.

150mm howitzers shell German positions across the Danube.

GIs of 45th Division carry their assault boat through the undergrowth to the riverbank.

the right; take the left turning after 300m for Marxheim (actually heading straight on) as the main road takes a sharp right across the River Danube.

Heading east through Altisheim and Leitheim, the road climbs the high ground overlooking the Danube valley to the right (the river lies hidden in the trees). 42nd Division crossed the river at this point on 26 April 1945, while 45th Division crossed at Marxheim. There are several opportunities to park and take in the spectacular views of the valley.

Marxheim is 9 miles from Donauworth. Turn right in the centre of the village and the road crosses the Danube after 600m. Parking is difficult and there is only a single parking space for a car on the far side of the bridge. Trees and undergrowth cover the banks where GIs once hauled assault boats down to the water's edge before paddling across the wide, fast flowing river.

Crossing the Danube

By nightfall on 25 April General Wade Haislip's XV Corps was in position on the north bank of the Danube, ready to cross the fast flowing river. Throughout the day his men had been carrying assault boats forward, taking advantage of the thick undergrowth along the riverbank, while lorries waited ready to carry bridging equipment down to the water's edge. The plan was to cross on a broad front under cover of darkness, in the hope of being able to strike south at the earliest opportunity. 42nd Division would cross immediately east of Donauworth, close to the confluence of the Danube and Lech Rivers, where hills on the north bank gave commanding views over the south bank. As one regiment expanded the bridgehead towards Donauworth, a second would bridge the Lech and meet up with a regiment of 45th Division, seizing the town of Rain. A second regiment of 45th Division would cross six miles to the east, where, again, the high ground on the north bank gave the American artillery the advantage. A later crossing between the two bridgeheads by the division's third regiment, timed to catch the Germans when they were fully engaged, would seal their fate. 20th Armoured Division would follow as soon as the bridgehead was secure and pass through the two divisions, heading southeast towards Munich.

42nd Division began to cross in assault boats shortly after midnight and General Harry Collins' plan to get as many men across while it was dark went as planned; it appeared that the Germans had not intended to defend the narrow promontory between the two rivers. On the division's right 232nd Regiment crossed at Altsheim and Leitheim and Colonel McNamee deployed his men ready to meet the anticipated counter-attacks at dawn. 1st Battalion led 242nd Regiment's crossing and again met no resistance on the southern shore. 3rd Battalion followed and headed for two bridges across the Lech River, hoping to seize them before they were destroyed and link up with 45th Division. However, they were too late, both bridges had been reduced to twisted wreckage.

As zero hour approaches the men anxiously watch for activity on the far side of the river.

The greatest difficulty faced by these men was getting into the boats without turning them over. Fortunately resistance was usually light but the swift current dragged many boats downstream.

20th Armoured Division wait under cover of smoke screen while 42nd Engineer Combat Battalion complete a treadway bridge.

A mounted anti-aircraft gun keeps guard over one crossing point as rafts take vehicles across the river.

The River Danube today.

Along the Danube 109th Engineer Battalion was busy operating ferries and building a treadway bridge while a thick smoke screen blinded the German artillery. By the afternoon tanks were pouring across, so fast that the southern end of the bridge collapsed under the weight of traffic; it was reopened for traffic by nightfall.

Although 42nd Division had crossed virtually unopposed, it was a completely different story in 45th Division's sector. Snipers and 20mm flak guns were waiting on the riverbank opposite 157th Regiment's sector, and the leading companies' assault boats were hit by heavy fire. Colonel O'Brien's men waded ashore to find infantry and self-propelled guns waiting for them in Niederschönenfeld. As mortars hit the river bank, the German observers correctly guessed that 157th Regiment's reserves would be passing through Marxheim and artillery shells and *nebelwerfer* rockets were soon raining down on the village, setting many buildings on fire. Despite the initial show of strength, before long the American artillery batteries were bringing down a concentrated barrage on the German positions, allowing the GIs to capture Niederschönenfeld, before pushing southeast towards Mittelstetten and Staudheim.

To the east 179th Regiment had to complete one final task before they could

The Danube; 'just another damn river'.

cross the river. German engineers had demolished the bridge in Neuburg late on 25 April, leaving many of their soldiers trapped on the north bank of the Danube. It left them in a hopeless situation and following a brief firefight, Colonel William Grace's men had rounded up the stragglers. The river bank was only lightly defended in the Regiment's sector and although small arms and artillery fire hit the assault boats as they crossed, Colonel Grace's men had soon swept all resistance aside, and taken Unterhausen and Oberhausen before turning their attentions on Neuburg.

While the Germans battled at the two crossing sites, 180th Regiment waited in the woods around Bertoldsheim for their turn to cross. By midday it was clear that the time to strike was drawing near and General Frederick gave Lieutenant-Colonel Everett Duvall the order to cross, starting at 15:00 hours.

Thick smoke screen drifted down the river as the GIs crossed but apart from the fast current and engine problems with some of the boats, the assault went as planned. As hoped, the Germans were not expecting the attack and as 3rd Battalion captured Strass village, 1st Battalion entered Burgheim and Ortfling. The new crossing had thrown the Germans into disarray and they soon realised that the river position had been lost, units then began to withdraw towards Schrobenhausen to the southeast.

The next task was get the 20th Armoured Division across so it could pursue the Germans towards Munich and the 1101st Engineer Group had the task of organising the ferries and bridgeworks along XV Corps' front. A second treadway bridge, a heavy pontoon bridge and a cable system for guiding DUKWs across were soon completed but plans to build a footbridge had to be abandoned because of the fast moving current. By midnight 45th Division had eight battalions of infantry across the river and they had secured a three kilometres deep bridgehead; the whole division would be across before dawn, leaving the way open for the 20th Armoured Division.

Crossing the River Lech

Although the river was a lot narrower than the Danube, the current was too fast to use assault boats and, to make matters worse, German troops had been spotted waiting behind the flood banks on the far side. Patrols believed that men could clamber across one of the wrecked bridges if the engineers could repair two small sections. 142nd Engineer's Company B got the short straw and they were called up to survey the wreckage, ready to start work as soon as it was dark. At nightfall men crawled out onto the structure and built a narrow gangplank as flares lit up the sky and bullets ricocheted off the steelwork. Miraculously only a handful were wounded and when the engineers withdrew at midnight the Germans believed that they had given up. They had not and one-by-one, 2nd Battalion quietly filed across and silenced a number of German outposts before the alarm was raised. The rest of the battalion had soon crossed and turned south to widen the bridgehead while 3rd Battalion followed and attacked the village of Rain. By morning the whole Regiment had crossed and engineers had started work on a treadway bridge.

Directions from the Danube to the River Lech

Continue south from the Danube and turn right at the roundabout after 2¹/₂ miles onto Route 16, heading for Donauworth. After 1 mile park in the layby to the right; and walk onto the bridge over the River Lech, noting how fast the current is. The Germans had blown both this bridge and the railway bridge to the south and 42nd Division's engineers had to work under fire to build a narrow walkway. Once the GIs had crossed they fanned out along the left hand bank and moved into Rain to meet 45th Division.

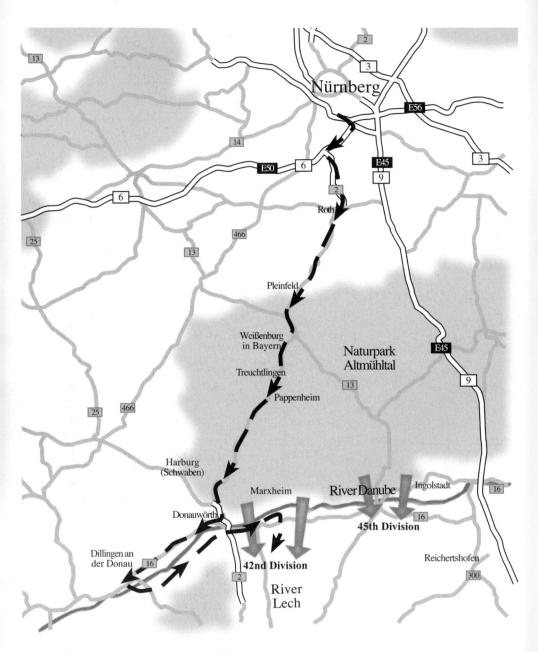

Directions to the Danube and the Letch.

Nürnberg

Roth

Pleinfeld

Weißenburg
in Bayern

Treuchtlingen

Pappenheim

Naturpark
Altmühltal

Harburg
(Schwaben)

Marxheim

River Danube

Ingolstadt

Donauwörth

45th Division

Dillingen an
der Donau

42nd Division

Reichertshofen

River
Lech

Chapter Eight

THE ROAD TO MUNICH

SLOW PROGRESS WAS MADE by XV Corps throughout the morning of 27 April as it pushed south from the Danube. Once 157th Regiment met 232nd Regiment at Gempfing, linking the two bridgeheads either side of the River Lech, 45th Division could concentrate on strengthening its hold east of the river. After clearing Neuburg, 179th Regiment pushed southeast, finding aircraft, petrol tankers and a large amount of ammunition abandoned on an airfield. Progress was slow in 180th Regiment's sector. Lightly armed German rearguards manned roadblocks as the main units withdrew towards Munich. It was a costly strategy for the Germans as nearly 4,000 soldiers were taken prisoner. By nightfall, General Haislip was confident that his bridgehead across the Danube was secure. With three bridges already open for traffic, 20th Armoured Division could begin to cross.

The advance began in earnest on the morning of 28 April. 20th Armoured Division took over the centre of XV Corps' front as 45th Division advanced on the flanks mounted on tanks, tank destroyers, artillery tows and lorries; the race for Munich was on.

On the south flank, poor roads hampered 157th Regiment's advance. Damaged bridges were continually bringing the advance to a halt and the engineers were kept busy carrying out temporary repairs. One task force intercepted and destroyed a column of German trucks and wagons near Grosshausen but elsewhere resistance was negligible. The Regiment billeted five miles north of Dachau later that night, unaware of the horrors that were about to unfold.

To the north, 179th Regiment advanced quickly. 1st Battalion led the way, riding on 106th Cavalry Group's armoured cars and jeeps while the rest of Colonel Grace's men followed mounted on the divisional artillery's transport. German infantry and self-propelled guns were seen dug in at Pfaffenhoffen and 1st Battalion dismounted while the reconnaissance vehicles withdrew to safety. With no tanks of his own to call on, Colonel Grace ordered the battalion to bypass the German position and cut their escape route towards Munich. The Germans withdrew later that night.

In the centre of 45th Division's sector, 180th Regiment continued its advance at first light but before long Colonel Duvall gave the order to pull over to let 20th Armoured Division past. The GIs welcomed the halt and looked forward

20th Armoured Division was soon heading at speed across open rolling countryside. Anything that moved was utilised as transport during the race towards Munich.

to a well-earned rest as the endless columns of tanks and halftracks rolled by. Major-General Orlando Ward planned to drive fast across country and his plan was designed to give his Task Force commanders maximum flexibility. Each Combat Command organised two small Task Forces and they were ordered to move as fast as possible on a broad front, limiting the number of vehicles on each road. Ward wanted to be able to switch roads with the minimum of congestion if the Germans started to destroy bridges.

Combat Command B organised two small Task Forces using 20th Tank Battalion's Shermans and 65th Armoured Infantry Battalion mounted in halftracks. They left Burgheim at first light and, after squeezing past 45th Division, Colonel Newton Jones' men headed southeast towards their first objective, the Paar Stream.

Task Force 65 moved quickly to Horzhausen only to find that the German engineers had already destroyed every bridge in the area. Although the infantry could wade across the stream, the tanks and halftracks were stranded on the north bank. On the north flank Task Force 20 found German rearguards waiting at Schrobenhausen. The infantry was forced to dismount and as they pushed forward on foot, the Germans destroyed the bridges one by one. The Task Force seized 100 prisoners and found two military hospitals, but the news that General Ward wanted to hear took time to filter through. The German engineers had overlooked a minor bridge and it was capable of carrying tanks. 20th Armoured Division was across the Paar. While 220th Armoured Engineer Battalion moved up to build new bridges, Task Force 20 crossed the Paar in single file as Task Force 65 queued up behind.

Directions to Schrobenhausen

From the Lech River retrace your route east along Route 16, bypassing Rain and turn left for Burgheim after 5 miles. Turn right at the end of the slip road and then left in the centre of the village, signposted for Ingolstadt. At the far end of the market place, take the right fork for Sinning. The road winds across the rolling countryside as it passes through Ortlfing and Dezenacker; turn right for Schrobenhausen at the T-junction just after St Wolfgang (5 miles from Burgheim). Continue straight on at the staggered crossroad for Schrobenhausen and pass through Hollenbach, turning left just beyond Dinkelshausen. There are spectacular views of the rolling wooded hills of northern Bavaria as you head towards Schrobenhausen nine miles away.

Head straight on for Stadtmitte, before turning right onto Regensburgerstrasse. Carry straight on at lights and cross the cobbled market place, heading straight on at the roundabout at the far end and cross the narrow River Parr.

German engineers blew all but one of the bridges around Schrobenhausen.

The Advance towards Munich

The two Task Forces fanned out on the south bank of the Paar Stream and they were soon back on their allotted roads and moving southeast towards the Gerols Stream. 33rd Cavalry Reconnaissance Squadron led the way, springing ambushes and locating roadblocks in their fast moving jeeps and armoured cars, so that the Task Forces could move quickly. A *panzerfaust* knocked out one armoured car as it slowed to squeeze past a roadblock in Aresing but the rearguard withdrew when 20th Tank Battalion's M5 Stuarts arrived. In the other villages the reconnaissance vehicles were often met by a display of white flags, a sign that the German soldiers had already fled.

Resistance was turning out to be minimal. The German rearguards were spread thin to cover all the roads, and many did not realise they had been bypassed until 20th Armoured Division's main body moved up. Task Force 65 had taken nearly 400 prisoners by the time it reached Gerolsbach. There was scattered small arms fire in the village but the Reconnaissance Squadron took the risk and raced forward to seize the bridge across the Gerols Stream before the German engineers could act. General Ward's plan was working; one Task Force was moving faster than the Germans thought possible. It meant that the chances of them blocking the road were declining by the hour.

It was a similar story on the road to Peterhausen and Task Force 65 crossed the Ilm and Glonn Streams in quick succession. French and Polish prisoners of war cheered the Americans on as they rolled into Peterhausen and they were eager to point out that a large German supply column had just left the village. It was too good an opportunity to pass up and Captain Heiler's M5 Stuart tanks set off in hot pursuit. They did not have far to go. The tanks met the column just beyond the village and Heiler's men opened fire with their cannons and machine guns. The German soldiers scattered for cover but the horse-drawn wagons and lorries had nowhere to hide and over fifty were torn to pieces. 150 prisoners were rounded up and sent to the rear as Task Force 65 threaded their way through the tangle of wrecked wagons and injured horses.

The Task Force then turned south onto Reichsstrasse 13 and seized four minor bridges over the River Amper before moving into Grossnobach. Engineers were putting the final touches to their explosives on the main bridge in the town when Task Force 65 approached with guns blazing. The heavy fire sent them running for cover as the tanks and halftracks drove across the last major barrier before Munich.

As the men dug in that night they could look back on the day with satisfaction. They had covered fifty miles, crossed four streams, and taken over

This German column met a grisly end when American reconnaissance troops caught up with it.

A squad rushes across a stream in pursuit of a German rearguard. The body of a German defender lies in the shallows.

1,200 prisoners. Munich was only ten miles away but after the experience at Nuremberg, no one expected the days ahead to be easy; the Nazis might be beaten but the battles were not over and everyone just hoped they would survive to see the end of the war.

29 April started badly for Combat Command B. Task Force 65 could see white flags in the tiny hamlet of Bioerbeck on the banks of the Amper River. However, as the reconnaissance vehicles slowed to squeeze past a roadblock, a trap was sprung. SS soldiers fired machine guns and *panzerfausts* from the houses, forcing the jeeps and armoured cars to withdraw. The Task Force commander was taking no chances and he ordered the self propelled howitzers at the rear of the column to move up and shell the hamlet. High explosive rounds ripped the small buildings to pieces while white phosphorus turned the ruins into burning tombs. However, the SS soldiers had fulfilled their mission. As the self-propelled artillery finished its work, German engineers blew the bridge over the Amper sky high. The Task Force's route was blocked.

Meanwhile, Task Force 20 was not having an easy time either at Lohnhof. Hidden 88s spotted the queue of vehicles as they waited for a tank dozer (a Sherman with bulldozer blade welded to the front) to clear roadblocks south of the village; four tanks had been knocked out before the column could pull

Gunfire sends the men diving for cover on the far bank.

The squad leader calls out targets as his men return fire.

The lightly armed SS rearguards stood no chance against the American Task Force's firepower.

back to safety. The Headquarters Company was ambushed as it waited in Lohnhof and crossfire hit many GIs before they could clamber off the tanks. As the leading halftracks drove through the gauntlet of fire with all guns blazing, the rest of the Company dismounted and attacked on foot. Many of the SS soldiers fought to the death and a sniper killed Colonel Newton Jones as he supervised the assault.

It had been a long day and as the weary GIs dug in for the night, their new commander, Colonel Edwin Carns settled down to plan the attack on their next objective; the SS-*Leibstandarte* Barracks, the largest SS barracks in Germany. Meanwhile, to the west advance troops from 45th and 42nd Divisions had reached the town of Dachau and uncovered horrific scenes in a huge concentration camp nearby.

Directions to Dachau

Continue through Aresing, signposted for Dachau, and turn left for Peterhausen at the far end of the village. Beyond the woods pass through Gerolsbach, turning right for Peterhausen at the far end of the village and cross the Gerol stream. The road meanders for 9 miles through small villages. After crossing the Ilm stream in Jetsondorf and passing through Peterhausen, turn left turn at the T-junction and cross the Glonn River. Continue through Kollbach, and Kammerberg, turning right onto Route 13 and Munchen in Fahrenhausen. Head south for 8 miles and turn right onto Route 471 for Dachau. Follow the 471 through Oberschleissheim into the outskirts of Dachau. Continue straight on at the first roundabout then turn right at the traffic lights into the industrial zone. The camp with its guard towers and perimeter wall is to the left after one mile. A large steel sculpture in the shape of an execution post stands opposite the car park.

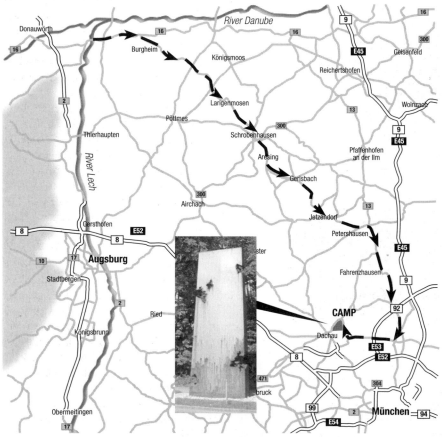

Inset: The symbolic execution post stands opposite Dachau's car park.

Chapter Nine

DACHAU CONCENTRATION CAMP

T HE NSDAP'S SCHUTZSTAFFEL, or SS protective squadron, was formed from the elite of Hitler's supporters in 1925. The organisation expanded to include surveillance, persecution and eventually included military units. Heinrich Himmler became the head of the SS in 1929 and its presence grew under his command, taking precedence over the SA after the Röhm Putsch in 1934. The concentration camps were run and guarded by a section of the SS and one of Dachau's commandants, Theodor Eicke, went on to head the Inspectorate for the Concentration Camps, introducing his brutal administrative system to the whole camp system. Himmler combined the State's Secret Police (Gestapo), the Criminal Police, the Uniformed Police and the Security Service of the SS, into one organisation, the Reich Security Main Office, and in 1939 the RSHA installed its regime into all aspects of life across Germany.

Dachau opened on 22 March 1933 and although the camp was run under existing prison regulations to begin with, new rules were introduced in October 1933. The guards could execute a prisoner without warning if he tried to escape or resisted (they could be handed over to the Political Police or dismissed from the SS if they refused). Prisoners could also be placed in the prison block and tortured for serious misdemeanours while minor infringements of the camp rules would result in their rations being cut, a ban on mail and punishment drills.

Theodor Eicke took command of Dachau on 26 June 1933 and ran it for just over a year introducing the extreme methods of treatment that were to become standard. He went on to form and command the Totenkopf Division.

Political opponents to the Nazi Party were the first group of prisoners incarcerated in the camp.

The Camp Administration

The camp staff were organised into five divisions under Eicke:

Department I: The Headquarters Department controlled the camp and issued disciplinary measures against prisoners and guards; it also ran the mail censorship office. The Chief of Staff dealt with the administrative side of the camp and carried out the commandant's orders.

Department II: The Political Department dealt with the admission and release of prisoners and controlled interrogations and police records.

Department III: The Prisoner Camp Department had two sections of guards. One ran the barrack area and the other supervised work inside and outside the camp. Both utilised prisoners to run the barrack blocks (called Stuben) and work details (called Capos).

Department IV: The Administration staff monitored the camp's budget and bought in clothes, food and equipment; they also 'looked after' the prisoners' possessions.

Above and left: 'Arbeit Macht Frei' – Work Brings Freedom. The motto cast into the wrought ironwork gate.

Right: Towers manned by armed guards surrounded the camp.

Right above: Prisoners were subjected to beatings and torture in the prison block.

Below: Robert Ley, head of the German Labour Front, inspects the Dachau guards.

Department V: The Medical Department's camp doctor ran an infirmary but few prisoners received any care. He was usually busy completing death certificates.

Barrack Area

A large SS barracks was established to the west of the prisoner camp and new Death's Head recruits were sent to Dachau to be trained and indoctrinated before they were transferred to other camps. When Theodor Eicke became inspector of the concentration camp system, many of his former subordinates were promoted to run their own camps and the 'Dachau system' had soon been spread across Nazi occupied Europe.

During the war years, many guards were transferred to the Waffen SS, to fight at the front and they had to be replaced by convalescing soldiers who were unfit for combat duty. The expansion of the sub-camp system also required extra guards and new recruits were brought in from conquered territories.

The administration building and barracks surround the parade ground. Prisoners were escorted through the gate at the bottom of the picture to work in the factory buildings.

Barracks

Commandant's House

Factories

Factories

Prison compound

Camp Leaders

Heinrich Himmler had a personal interest in the Dachau concentration camp. As he rose from Chief of the Munich Police and commander of the political police in Bavaria in 1933 to *Reichsminister* of the interior in 1943, the *Reichsführer* of the SS was personally responsible for choosing the camp commandants.

The Commandant's house opposite the camp gate. Note the sentry box.

Hilmar Wäckerle took over in April 1933 and had four prisoners shot on his second day in command. At this time the police were obliged to 'investigate' the circumstances surrounding their deaths and Wäckerle was dismissed from his post, however, he still continued to serve in the SS. The Munich lawyer, Karl Wintersberger, persisted in investigating the deaths until he was removed from his post; the cases were then closed.

Theodor Eicke took over in June 1933 and his organisation skills did not go unnoticed; Himmler promoted him to head all the concentration camps at the end of 1934. The Guard units were given the title SS Death's Head units in 1936 and three years later, Eicke took command of the SS Death's Head (*Totenkopf*) Division. He led the division throughout the French and Russian campaigns (during which the unit became notorious for murdering prisoners) until his death in a plane crash in February 1943.

Eicke's replacement, Heinrich Deubel, only lasted eighteen months. Many did not like his relaxed regime and longed to return to Eicke's brutal methods and after he was accused of misappropriation of funds and other misdemeanours, he left and returned to his former occupation, a customs official.

Hans Loritz had worked at Dachau under Eicke and when he returned as commandant in April 1936 he went out of his way to 'improve' on his former leader's excesses, encouraging harsh treatment of the prisoners. He left in December 1939 and went on to command the Norwegian concentration camps. Loritz committed suicide when the war came to an end.

Alex Piorkowski had worked under Loritz for over a year and as a former member of Himmler's personal staff, he was an ideal candidate. He was promoted to lead the camp in September 1939 and he made sure that thousands of Polish prisoners were treated badly and supervised the execution of 4,000 Russian prisoners of war. He was accused of corruption in the summer of 1942 and was dismissed from the SS a year later. He was tried at Dachau after the war and later executed.

Martin Weiss had been the camp adjutant for some time when he became commandant in September 1942. He immediately murdered anyone who was too ill to work to make way for new prisoners. Weiss transferred to Lublin-Majdanek concentration camp twelve months later and was executed after the war.

Eduard Weiter took over in November 1943. He showed little interest in the camp and let his subordinates deal with the day to day running. Thousands died of malnutrition and disease under his command and he fled as the Americans closed in. Weiter committed suicide a few days later.

Layout of the Camp

The prisoners lived in the abandoned buildings of Dachau munitions plant when the camp opened in March 1933. There were ten stone barracks, each containing 250 prisoners living in cramped dormitories. The prisoners tore down the old buildings in 1936 to make way for a new model camp, one that would set the standard across Nazi occupied Europe.

Gatehouse (*Jourhaus*)

Prisoners were welcomed to Dachau with the words *Arbeit Macht Frei* cast into the wrought ironwork gate of the Gatehouse (*Jourhaus*). The words translate as Work brings Freedom, a hollow promise to the prisoners incarcerated in Dachau, where the only freedom was death from overwork, starvation, disease or at the hands of the brutal guards.

The rooms to the left of the gate housed the Guard Officer and Guardroom, while the Duty Officer registered new prisoners in the room to the right. The Gestapo and protective custody camp leaders occupied the offices on the top floor.

The entrance to the prison camp.

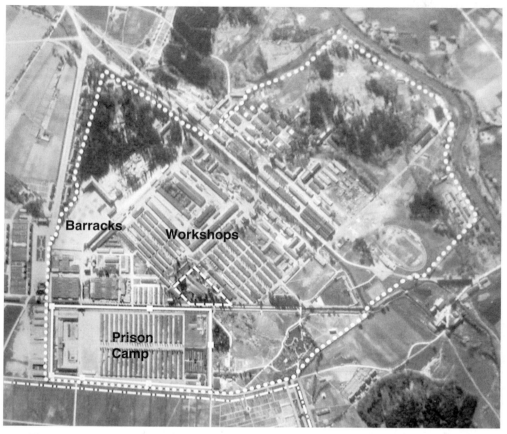

Barracks

Workshops

Prison Camp

The Dachau complex covered a large area, with the prison camp taking up a small area alongside the barracks and the workshops.

Below: A section of the ditch and the electric fence have been preserved.

The prisoners soon realised that Dachau was hidden from the outside world by a series of impenetrable barriers. Anyone stepping on the strip of grass surrounding the compound would be shot by any of the guards in the watchtowers or patrolling the perimeter, before they could reach the water-filled ditch (*Graben*). An electric fence (*Stacheldrahthindernis*) was waiting for anyone the guards missed, and many chose to commit suicide by running for the fence. The final barrier, a high concrete wall, made sure that no one could see in, or out, of the compound. Escape was impossible.

Administration Building (*Wirtschaftsgebaude*)

The long elongated building to the right of the entrance housed many of the camp's administration functions. It was completed in 1938 and is now home to the Museum. It is filled with artifacts and photographs depicting life in the camp and the cold bare walls are a stark reminder of the terror inflicted on the prisoners during their internment.

The west wing was filled with workshops and prisoners employed on maintenance duties around the camp used the rooms. New arrivals had been harassed and beaten as they were herded towards the camp and by the time they reached the building they were well aware that Dachau was a violent place. After registration they were given a lecture on camp rules and regulations as they handed over their clothing and personal belongings.

The naked prisoners were then driven into the showers, passing the Boiler Room (it only provided heating for the *Jourhaus* and the maintenance building, the barracks were unheated) and the Disinfecting Room, where clothes were cleaned. Heads were shaved in the corridor in front of the showers before the prisoners were given their blue and white striped uniform. With their identity gone and replaced by a number, the bewildered men were escorted to their barrack block to begin the daily grind of camp life.

Prisoners were showered weekly to begin with and the guards delighted in harassing them as they tried to get clean. As the number of prisoners rose, showers increasingly became a luxury and in 1941 the room was turned into a

The Administration Building stands in front of the square where the prisoners paraded for roll call twice a day; punishments were often carried out in front of the men.

place of torment. Prisoners had been subjected to pole hanging (a brutal torture where the prisoners' arms were twisted behind their back before they were suspended for several hours) since the early days. Men were hung from the shower room beams in groups, often while guards hit or spun the suspended men as others cheered them on. For the sick, the showers were their last glimpse of Dachau as they waited for transports to take them to Hartheim castle near Linz where they would be gassed.

The east wing of the building housed the kitchens and the food stores. Another room contained large drum washing machines to wash the prisoners' clothes.

The large open area in front of the Administration Building served as a parade ground and as prisoners lined up for the roll call, they could see the motto painted in large white letters on the roof staring down at them:

There is only one road to freedom. Its milestones are: obedience, diligence, honesty, orderliness, cleanliness, sobriety, truthfulness, self-sacrifice, and love of the Fatherland.

The Barracks (*Wohnbaracken*)

After 1936 the prisoners lived in thirty-four identical wooden barrack buildings either side of the main camp road (*Lagerstrasse*). Every day work details cleaned the camp and one detail levelled the gravel road with a huge roller. Two rows of poplar trees alongside the road and flowerbeds at the end of each building gave the camp an air of respectability.

The first four buildings were designated B to E (the Administration Building was Building A). Block B was the camp canteen (*Kantine*) where prisoners could buy cigarettes and extra food with camp money; extra money could be sent by the family and converted into the camp currency at an exorbitant rate. A small stock of books was kept in Block C, the Camp library. The Social Democrat politician Kurt Schumacher opened it in the autumn of 1933 and he held secret political meetings in the building using books smuggled into the camp.

Buildings D and E were used as the camp hospital (*Revierbaracken*) and part of building E served as the mortuary (*Totenkammer*); three extra barrack buildings were turned into infirmaries when typhus and dysentery spread throughout the camp. The nurses had no medical knowledge and the custody camp leader decided if a prisoner could see the SS camp doctor. Few received treatment and medical care was negligible. A typhoid epidemic swept through the camp during the final months of the war and American troops found Blocks 1 to 11 filled with the sick and dying men when they liberated the camp.

SS soldiers were appointed as block leaders to begin with but as the numbers of prisoners grew they appointed prisoners as block and room leaders, known as *Stuben*. Each block had a secretary, a barber and a canteen

The barrack blocks flanked the camp road.

manager, while apartment seniors were appointed to run each room; they all reported to the block senior. The *Stuben* were usually chosen for their brutality and willingness to adhere to orders. They were rewarded for keeping their block clean and orderly; they would be dismissed or punished if they failed to meet SS leaders' standards. Many prisoners testified against their former block leaders when they were brought to trial after the war.

The remaining barrack buildings each housed 208 prisoners, split into four rooms with a day room and dormitories; a washroom and toilet facilities served each pair of dormitory. The prisoners slept on open sided timber beds, stacked three tiers high. The day room only had a few benches and tables. The camp rules forbade anyone from lying on the beds until lights out so everyone else had to stand. Prisoners had to keep their block immaculate and what little free time they had was dedicated to cleaning the floors and lockers ready for the next inspection.

Blocks 2 and 4 housed German prisoners while Barrack 9 was used to quarantine new arrivals. Doctors used Block 5 for medical experiments as part of the Reich Research Program after March 1941. A range of barbaric tests were organised by Dr Siegfried Ruff and Professor Holzlöhner and many of their victims died. Some were injected with malaria or tuberculosis so the symptoms could be studied while new antidotes were tested. Tests designed to aid the jet fighter programme involved prisoners being subjected to low pressures, usually until the victim died. The *Luftwaffe* also asked for hypothermia tests where prisoners were immersed in cold water until they passed out; over ninety died.

Jewish prisoners lived in Block 15, and Blocks 17 and 19 were known as the penal blocks (*Strafblöcke*) housing repeat offenders. The three blocks were separated from the rest of the camp by a barbed wire fence and the prisoners were forbidden from using the canteen, the library and the brothel. They were also singled out for punishments and severe work details.

In 1940 over 13,375 Polish citizens were sent to Dachau. The Polish clergymen were isolated from the rest in Blocks 26, 28, and 30; they continued to celebrate mass in Block 26. Block 30 was eventually used to house the sick. A camp brothel was set up behind Block 29 in April 1944 but the majority of prisoners chose to ignore it.

Following the typhus epidemic in 1943, a barrack was set up in the garden area behind Block 29, where prisoners as well as clothing and blankets were disinfected. The guards avoided the building for fear of infection and prisoners used it to hold secret meetings.

The Crematorium Area

A crematorium area was built just outside the camp perimeter in 1940 to help stop the spread of disease. It had a small half-timbered cabin with a furnace, and a warehouse for storing bodies. Barrack X with four furnaces was opened nearby in April 1943 to cope with the rise in deaths; it also had an area to disinfect clothing.

The centre of Barrack X had a gas chamber with ante-rooms and although it was designed to exterminate prisoners, it is believed that only a few prisoners were murdered by gassing. The intention was to usher prisoners through the entrance into the waiting room before they stripped in the disrobing room. A small gas chamber beyond had air-tight doors and small openings on the wall where guards would place the Zyklon B pellets. Showerheads in the ceiling kept up the pretence of showering until the prisoners' final moments. After the prisoners had been gassed, the far door opened into the mortuary room and a work detail prepared the bodies for cremation. The working detail was kept separate from the rest of the camp, so that the horrors of Barrack X could be kept secret. They lived in a small room behind the crematorium and they would be killed when they were no longer fit to work.

The four crematorium ovens were in constant operation for the next two years, disposing of around 300 bodies a month, rising to 4,000 a month by the time they were shut down in February 1945 when coal stocks ran out. There was a second mortuary room beyond the crematorium room.

45th Division's GIs came across the crematorium area as they advanced towards the prison camp and they were shocked by the sights they discovered in and around the building. Sergeant Scott Corbett, a writer for 42nd Division's newspaper, the *Rainbow Reveille*, later described what they found:

> In the crematorium, the skeleton-like bodies of the dead still lay in a room next to the furnace, stacked like cordwood. The cement floor slanted to a drain which carried off the blood, but not the unforgettable stench of death.

General Eisenhower made sure that thousands of GIs and senior officials came to see what his men had uncovered at Barrack X to make sure that no one would forget the horrors perpetrated here.

Life in the Camp

Prisoners were threatened and beaten as they were dragged off their transport and marched or driven to the camp. A bus service was introduced in November 1937 and in later years arrivals were delivered to the front gate by train on a new railway siding. After handing over their personal effects, prisoners were showered and issued with their striped uniform. Some were singled out and tied to a whipping stool where guards administered twenty-five blows with a bullwhip; it was the first sign that Dachau was not a regular prison.

Barrack X, the Crematorium Building.

Living conditions were always oppressive, and the prisoners had to live in daily fear of punishments, torture and random beatings. The SS guards stepped up the violence after 1936 and a directive issued by the Secret State Police Office in September 1939 allowed the guards to impose death sentences after making a short application to the *Reichsführer* SS. During this period violence against the prisoners reached its peak.

Over 35,000 prisoners were held at Dachau from the time it opened in 1933 until it was temporarily closed in 1939. Although many prisoners were released, over 500 had died. Most wore a regular shirt and striped prison pants with their number sewn on the leg. The category of prisoners held in Dachau concentration camp varied considerably over the years. Each prisoner wore a coloured badge on their uniform to denote their 'crime'.

Political opponents and a small number of Jewish prisoners came first. Communists, Social Democrats, anarchists, and other enemies of the state had to wear a red triangle while the Jewish badge was a yellow triangle (the yellow star appeared later).

The next group of prisoners arrived later in the year after the Nazis introduced laws where every able-bodied male citizen had to take a job and could not leave without permission. The Gestapo rounded up the work-shy, vagrants, prostitutes, alcoholics, beggars, anti-socials, criminals and the homeless and sent them to Dachau. They wore black triangles and were assigned the hardest tasks. Professional criminals followed in 1935 and they wore green triangular patches. Foreign forced labourers wore blue triangles while red triangles marked with the letter P singled out Polish political prisoners.

Many prisoners were released when they had been 'rehabilitated'; but they still had to report to the local police on a daily basis. Re-offenders found themselves in the penal colony. A bar was sewn over the triangle to indicate a second offender while a black circle beneath denoted the penal colony. They were withheld privileges and usually worked in the gravel pit or the quarry.

It had been an offence to be a Jehovah's Witness since 1933 and in 1935 the Nazis took action as members refused to join the armed forces or give the Hitler salute. Police action put thousands in jail and 2,500 were eventually sent to concentration camps. A large number ended up in Dachau where they were singled out with a purple triangular patch. In the same year homosexuals were targeted as foreign to the community and over 600 were brought to Dachau. Their pink triangular patch attracted special attention from the guards and they were subjected to violent humiliation.

As the Nazi regime increased its grip on society, many feared for their lives and fled to other countries to escape persecution. A few were expelled and sent back to Germany while others returned of their own accord. After 1935, returning emigrants were arrested and sent to a concentration camp; they had to wear a blue triangular patch.

A railway siding was added later so that prisoners could be brought to the camp gates.

Armed guards escort new arrivals to the camp.

The gypsy groups known as the Sinti and the Roma had been targeted since 1933 and laws restricting their movement had driven many into internment camps. The Nuremberg Racial Laws of 1935 excluded them from society and they were rounded up in 1938. Branded as anti-socials to begin with, the gypsies later had to wear a brown triangular badge. They were moved en-masse to Mauthausen Camp in August 1938 where many died in the quarries.

The Daily Regime

The day started with Reveille at 04:00 hours (5:00 hours in the winter) and for the next hour the prisoners made their beds and cleaned their barracks; untidiness was rewarded with punishment. By 05:15 hours every man was standing in silence and to attention on the parade ground waiting his turn to answer the roll call. It took

nearly an hour to complete. Punishments were often carried out after the roll call in front of the prisoners.

The men were then split into work details and the *capos* were allowed to mete out their own beatings while the SS guards looked on. To begin with the SS organised pointless tasks, such as moving piles of rocks backwards and forwards, to break the prisoners' spirit. The guards sometimes ordered them to work at the run, beating anyone who could not keep up. Work details were soon given productive work, and groups of prisoners were escorted out of the camp to carry out mundane maintenance tasks. In 1936 work started on demolishing the old buildings, replacing them with new barrack blocks. Others worked on the plantation just outside the camp, while the gravel pit was a feared place reserved for the penal colony and Jewish prisoners.

After working from 06:00 hours (dawn during winter months) until midday, the work parties were marched back to the camp and fed with a small piece of bread and a bowl of thin soup. The amount of calories was minimal but the meagre ration was repeatedly cut during the war years. The parties had to be back at work by 13:00 hours and work continued until 18:30 hours (nightfall in the winter), the men were then marched back to the camp for evening roll call. Another bland meal, sometimes with a small lump of sausage or cheese added, was followed by a scramble to clean up the barrack room before lights out at 21:00 hours.

There was little free time and it was impossible to organise resistance against the guards. Contact with the outside world was extremely limited and prisoners were barred from receiving visitors while letters were heavily censored. Even so a few brave men smuggled out news from time to time, risking torture or death if they were caught.

In October 1933 the 'Disciplinary and Punishment Regulations for the Prisoner Camp' laid down strict rules but the guards continued their regime of punishment and torture, falsifying death certificates to cover up murders. Torture methods knew no bounds. Some men were made to stand to attention or squat for hours while others were taken to the prison block and kept in solitary confinement, often chained up in the dark with no food or water. Pole hanging was often carried out in the prison enclosure or the showers. Many were tied to a wooden trestle and whipped with a bullwhip as the prisoner counted the blows aloud; any mistakes and the punishment started again. In 1940 SS-*Hauptsturmführer* Zill introduced a second guard so the two could whip the prisoner in unison.

Despite the fearsome beatings and tortures, the number of deaths in the first five years only averaged at around two per month. However, prisoners lived in constant fear and some committed suicide after suffering abuse while others were encouraged to end their life by the guards. Troublesome prisoners were sometimes 'shot while trying to escape'; in other words murdered.

The next large batch of prisoners arrived in 1938 and by November there were around 60,000 men in a camp that had been designed for 6,000. Living conditions deteriorated and the death toll leapt tenfold as the guards increased their brutality towards the prisoners; it was the start of an increasing trend of disease, overwork and violence.

German troops crossed the border into Austria on 13 March 1938 and the Gestapo followed. Austrian Nazi sympathisers had already drawn up lists of political opponents and thousands were rounded up in the weeks that followed. Many ended up in Dachau. Similar action was taken following the occupation of the Czechoslovakian border area in October and 5,500 Sudeten men found themselves in the German concentration camps. Over 100 officials from the Czech town of Kladno were brought to Dachau as a reprisal for the shooting of a German policeman.

There had always been a small number of Jews in the camp, many from Austria and Czechoslovakia but in September 1938 all 2,400 were transferred to Buchenwald concentration camp. They were soon replaced. The SA and SS went on the rampage on the night of 9 November 1938, burning synagogues, looting shops and arresting thousands of Jews. Following *Reichskristallnacht* (The Night of Broken Glass), 11,000 were incarcerated in Dachau and the guards went out of their way to make their lives a misery. They continued to wear the yellow triangle and a second coloured triangle was added if a prisoner was accused of any other crime (the yellow star was introduced in September 1941). Most were released a few weeks later, on the condition that they left Germany within six months, an impossible task.

Work details were suspended in the summer of 1939 following an outbreak of dysentery and in September the prisoners were transferred to Buchenwald, Flossenbürg and Mauthausen. The SS-*Totenkopf* (Death's Head) Division used the camp as a training facility over the winter and when the prisoners returned the following spring they found that conditions had dramatically deteriorated. Work was increased as the food decreased and the *capos* pushed the men until they dropped.

The whipping stool where prisoners were tied and lashed with the bullwhip.

Rauchen verboten

Smoking is forbidden! Dozens of rules dominated the prisoners' lives and the guards severely punished any transgression.

The number of deaths had soared to over 2,500 per year by 1941, the year when over 4,000 Russian prisoners of war were murdered in the nearby firing range. It again leapt to over 5,100 in 1942 as another 2,500 sick prisoners were taken to Hartheim Castle to be gassed. By the summer of 1942 the Nazis had decided on the fate of the Jews and trainloads were deported to the extermination camps in the east. The gypsies left at the same time, their fate sealed. A second typhoid outbreak claimed many lives over the winter but the spring of 1943 marked a change in the way that the camp operated.

German industry needed forced labour to help the war effort and prisoners would be worked until they died. The SS had exploited prison labour since 1942, sending work details to small camps around Munich where they worked in factories or in the city

The striped prison uniform with the number stitched on the trouser leg.

Roll call could take several hours.

A work detail strains as it pushes a wagon to the stone heap.

The camp road was a focal point in the centre of the prisoners' compound.

clearing up rubble after air raids. Allied air attacks were driving the German aviation industry out of the cities and many factories had been moved into large bunkers or tunnels in the country by the end of 1943. The *Luftwaffe* commissioned Organisation Todt to build the Kaufering complex as part of the *Jäger* program, a plan to build 3,000 fighter planes a month. 100,000 Jewish prisoners were eventually transported from camps to help build six huge concrete bunkers in the woods around Landsberg.

Dachau became the collection point for the influx of prisoners, holding them until the sub-camps called for a new batch. Living conditions at the Kaufering camps were terrible and the regimes were designed to work the prisoners to death. The sick were either returned to Dachau so they could be forwarded to Auschwitz extermination camp or sent to Lublin-Majdanek or Bergen-Belsen where they would be left to die.

The enforced labour system was in a state of collapse by the end of 1944, as typhus once again swept through the crowded camps. As the Allies advanced across Germany, the Nazis started to evacuate the camps, destroying them as they left, in the hope of hiding their terrible secret. Thousands of prisoners were force marched into the Alps; hounded by their guards and those who were too ill to keep up were killed or left to die along the roadside. As the Americans approached Munich at the end of April 1945, many of the camp guards fled, leaving the prisoners behind.

The Liberation

By the time American soldiers approached Dachau, there were around 40,000 prisoners crammed into the camp, many of them emaciated and dying from typhus. Hitler was determined that none of the prisoners would fall into Allied hands but only 10,000 had been evacuated by the time XV Corps closed in, the rest had been

A work detail stands in silence while they are counted.

crammed into the barracks and watched over by a small group of SS guards.

Two groups of SS soldiers reached Dachau on 28 April. Waffen-SS *Obersturmführer* Heinrich Skodzenski had occupied the barracks with his company of 200 soldiers. Meanwhile, SS-*Untersturmführer* Heinrich Wicker had spent April evacuating the small sub-camps around Munich. As the month drew to a close, Wicker was placed in command of *Kampfgrüppe Süd* and then ordered to take his 200 men to Dachau. He arrived on the night of 28 April only to find that *Kommandant* Weiter and many of the guards had fled so he decided to wait and surrender the camp to the approaching Americans.

An Oberscharführer *camp guard and his dog.*

Dr Victor Maurer, a Swiss Red Cross representative, had arrived the day before with five lorries filled with food. Maurer was concerned that the prisoners might take their revenge on the local population if they were set free and he persuaded Wicker to keep them under guard. After posting guards in the sentry towers, the rest of his men stacked their weapons and waited for the Americans to arrive.

Accounts of what happened in and around Dachau on the afternoon of 29 April are understandably confusing, but what is clear is that two units, one from the 42nd Division and one from the 45th Division reached different parts of the camp at around 16:30 hours.

In 45th Division's sector 157th Regiment's Company I realised all was not

Two of the barrack blocks have been rebuilt and furnished in their original style.

Lockers had to be spotless to avoid punishment.

The prisoners slept in uncomfortable wooden beds stacked three high.

Dozens of men had to wash at these two water fountains.

A cramped toilet room.

well when they came across a line of railway carriages abandoned on a siding, west of the camp. Lieutenant William Walsh's men were shocked to find that the carriages were filled with emaciated bodies, many with bullet wounds. Lieutenant Bill Cowling, a soldier serving with the 42nd Division, later wrote the following piece in a letter to his family:

> As we approached the camp the first thing we came to was a railroad track leading out of the camp with a lot of open box cars on it. As we crossed the tracks we looked back into the cars, and the most horrible sight I had ever seen met my eyes. The cars were loaded with dead bodies. Most of them were naked and all of them skin and bones ... Many of the bodies had bullet holes in the back of their heads. It made us sick at our stomachs and so mad but we could do nothing but clench our fists.

The train soon became known as the Death Train.

SS officer Hans Merbach had been ordered to escort the train from Buchenwald to Dachau on 7 April but 350 prisoners had already been shot by the time they reached Weimar railway station. The journey proved to be fraught with difficulties and the route changed constantly due to Allied bombing raids. Merbach's guards spent the journey carrying out random executions and shot civilians in the Czechoslovakian town of Pilsen when they tried to give food for the prisoners. At one stop he ordered the French prisoners off the train and killed them, shooting those too weak to dig graves. Without food or water, the prisoners huddled in the open wagons as they moved around Germany, and many were killed when Allied planes strafed the train. It had been on the move for nearly three weeks when it was abandoned at Dachau. The incensed American soldiers found the bodies where they had been left (numbers range from 500 to 2,000).

Obersturmführer Skodzenski met Walsh's men at the SS Barracks. Skodzenski intended to surrender his company but the incensed GIs shot him on the spot; four other men were also taken prisoner and killed. With feelings running high, Walsh's men continued through the barracks, finding that many of Skodzenski's men were willing to put up a fight.

The GIs had heard plenty of stories about *Waffen* SS soldiers showing American prisoners no mercy but they took their prisoners to the barracks coal yard and placed them under guard. According to some accounts a few soldiers tried to escape, others say they were executed. What is clear is that the soldier manning the machine gun opened fire on the group and a number had been shot before Colonel Felix Sparks intervened. After clearing the SS barracks, Walsh's men eventually reached the western perimeter fence of the prison camp where they met some 42nd Division soldiers.

Civilians and two newspaper reporters had told 42nd Division about the camp as it approached from the west and General Harry Collins had sent Brigadier-General Henning Linden forward with an advance party to investigate. Lieutenant Bill Cowling's jeep headed the small group and after passing the Death Train he headed towards the prison camp. He found the entrance at the southwest corner of the camp and warily entered, becoming the first American soldier to enter the prison enclosure:

We went through the gate into a large cement square surrounded by low black barracks and the whole area was enclosed by barbed wire. When we entered the gate not a soul was in sight. Then suddenly people (if you could call them that) came from all directions. They were dirty starved skeletons with torn clothes and they screamed, hollered and cried. They ran up and grabbed us and kissed our hands, our feet and all of them tried to touch us. They grabbed us and tossed us into the air screaming at the top of their lungs. I finally managed to pull myself free and get to the gate and shut it so they could not get out.

While Cowling explored the compound, General Linden found Dr Maurer, Wicker and his assistant waiting beneath a white flag outside the entrance to the SS barracks. After officially surrendering the camp, Wicker explained that while the majority of his guards were unarmed, he had posted armed guards in the towers surrounding the prison enclosure. With fighting still going on around the barracks, it was a delicate situation and Linden had few men to

Obviously infuriated by seeing the appalling state of the inmates of Dachau, the GI manning the machine gun has just opened fire on the line of captured German SS guards.

181

The entrance to the prison compound on the day of liberation.

deal with so many prisoners.

At 17:30 hours Linden's group reached the *Jourhus*, finding Cowling with eight of the guards. Colonel Sparks soon joined them and although the prisoners were pleading to be let out, Linden decided to keep them inside for their own safety. Chaotic scenes followed inside the compound and a few prisoners were killed by the electric fence as they reached through to greet their liberators. When shots rang out from Tower B (whether they were fired to warn the prisoners or at the Americans is unclear) men from 222nd Regiment's 1st Battalion moved in. The guards were killed in the gun battle that followed (some say during the gun battle, others say they were executed after they had surrendered).

With feelings running high, Linden took steps to relieve the rest of the SS guards, but sporadic fighting continued inside the camp until nightfall as the inmates set upon their *capos* and SS guards who had disguised themselves as prisoners.

The number of SS soldiers, either *Waffen* SS or SS guards killed on 29 April range from around 30 to over 120; many of them were attacked by enraged prisoners, (either beaten to death or with guns given to them by sympathetic GIs). Wicker was one of those killed and his body was never formally identified.

As 42nd Division took over responsibility for guarding the camp, 45th Division took up residence in the SS barracks. Meanwhile General Linden accompanied a group of journalists on a tour of the compound and met the International Prisoner Committee, putting it in temporary charge of the prisoner camp until the American authorities could take over.

Dachau After the Liberation

45th Division left 180th Regiment behind as it moved into Munich so that Colonel Duvall's men could start the process of helping the prisoners on their long road to recovery. Hundreds were still dying and engineers were drafted in to dig mass graves on nearby Leitenberg hill; over 2,300 were eventually taken there. Duvall made sure that the people of Dachau were involved so they would not forget.

Area Command Dachau was set up to deal with the immediate problems of housing, feeding and the health of the survivors, while teams of officers questioned the prisoners, gathering evidence of war crimes.

Prisoners started to leave as soon as they were healthy and the final group left in July 1945 but while many went home, others, mainly the Jewish internees, had no homes or families to return to. They were directed to resettlement camps so they could start to piece their lives back together and, in many cases, prepare for emigration.

The Military Government and the US Army's security service, (the CIC), arrested thousands of National Socialist leaders and members of the SS in the months following the end of the war. Dachau was named Internment Camp 29 towards the end of 1945 and over the next three years around 25,000 prisoners were held in the barracks.

An American military court was set up in the SS camp and they started with the Dachau staff. After hearing statements from prisoners, and seeing documents and photographs, thirty-six men were sentenced to death. Eight sentences were later reduced to prison terms but on 28 and 29 May 1946 twenty-eight members of the camp staff were executed.

Over the next three years the court held 489 trials hearing 1,672 individual cases. The accused included the staff from Mauthausen, Flossenbürg, Mühldorf, Mittelbau-Dora and Buchenwald concentration camps. Other members of the SS were also tried, including Otto Skorzeny and the men led by Joachim Peiper who were accused of murdering American prisoners near Malmedy during the Battle of the Bulge. Over 400 men and women were

The prisoners give a cheer for their liberators.

General Linden questions Wicker while Doctor Maurer listens.

General Linden tries to bring order to the chaos.

sentenced to death, another 1,000 were given prison sentences; the rest were acquitted. Attempts were made to re-educate the prisoners, but few had seen the error of their ways before they were released during the amnesties in the 1950s.

The Bavarian Refugee Agency took over the camp in September 1948 and the barracks were turned over to refugees, made homeless by the war. The camp would serve as home to thousands over the next seventeen years.

A Memorial Site

The crematorium compound has been used as an area of remembrance since 1945 and the unknown prisoner memorial was erected next to Barrack X in 1950. The combined efforts of many, led by Alois Hundhammer, Otto Kohlhofer, Bishop Johannes Neuhäusler, Ruth Jakusch and Father Leonard Roth, made sure that the camp became a place to visit and remember.

As the refugees started to leave in the mid 1960s, work started on the Memorial Site we see today. The barracks buildings were torn down and the poplar trees were removed in 1964. Blocks B and D were rebuilt the following year and opened to the public; new trees were planted in the 1980s. Thirty rectangular beds of gravel mark the site of blocks 1 to 30 and concrete markers along the roadside guide visitors around the camp. Memorials and monuments stand at each end of the huge open area.

The Catholic Chapel stands at the north end of the camp road. Dr Johannes Neuhäusler, the Bishop of Munich and a Dachau inmate instigated it. Josef Wiedemann's design is a tall circular concrete structure, adorned with a crown of thorns and a bell tower; wrought iron gates protect the open interior. 50,000

The entrance to the SS Barracks.

people attended the inauguration in August 1960 and soon afterwards Neuhäusler suggested building Protestant and Jewish Memorials.

The huge basalt Jewish Memorial was designed by Frankfurt architect Hermann Zwi Guttmann and it was dedicated on 7 May 1967. An iron fence, cast into the shape of barbed wire, lines the ramp down to the underground prayer room where the Hebrew inscription on the gate reads:

Give them a sign of warning, eternal one! The peoples should learn that they are mortals.

During the war angora rabbits had been bred in hutches behind the Memorial and their fur was used to line *Luftwaffe* uniforms. Heinrich Himmler took his daughter, Gudrun, to see the rabbits; a

GIs hand out candy and cigarettes to the prisoners.

For some the liberation came too late.

A GI inspects the entrance to the gas chamber.

bizarre touch of fatherly kindness at the camp.

The Protestant memorial is in the northwest corner, close to the site of the camp greenhouse and gardens. Helmut Striffler designed the underground church and the random design was a statement against the Nazis' obsession with order. It was dedicated on 30 April 1967.

The International Memorial stands in front of the Administration Building. A ramp zig-zags its way down to the foot of Nandor Glid's unforgettable bronze sculpture depicting skeletons hanging from a section of barbed wire fence. The memorial was dedicated in September 1968. A wall, inscribed with the words 'Never Again' in five languages, stands to the east of the memorial while a second wall to the west bears the inscription,

Stacks of bodies surrounded the crematorium.

The barracks serves as a centre for War Crimes Trials. Joachim Peiper sits in the chair. He is accused of involvement in murdering American prisoners near Malmedy during the Battle of the Bulge and received the death sentence, later commuted to imprisonment. He was released in December 1956 and was murdered in France, where he had made his home, in 1976.

May the example of those who were exterminated here between 1933 and 1945 because of their fight against National Socialism unite the living.

Visiting Dachau Concentration Camp

The entrance to the Dachau complex is at the far end of the car park. Beyond the side road is a series of information boards grouped around the information kiosk and bookshop. Entrance to the grounds is free and there are audio guides available for 3 euros (concessionary 2 euros). Details of the guided tour are available at the kiosk. Allow three hours to see everything and no one leaves Dachau unmoved, the place certainly has an eerie feel about it. Visitors can wander around the grounds and there are many information boards but the following guide covers the main points of interest.

Follow the gravel path beyond the information kiosk to the gatehouse, 200

The commandant's house has hardly changed; police now use the building.

metres on the right. Before entering the gate note the remains of the railway and platform to the left, installed so that trains could bring prisoners directly to the gate. Through the fence beyond the platform is the commandant's house and the SS Barracks where guards were taught the 'Dachau System' before they were posted to camps across Europe.

Pass through the gate, noting the liberation plaques on the walls. The words *Arbeit Macht Frei, Work brings Freedom,* cast into the gate frames the open parade ground where prisoners stood for roll call. Start your visit in the Administration Block to the right of the gate where there are exhibits, film shows and photographs. There are several international memorials in front of the Block.

The Penal Yard and Prison Block are behind the Administration Block. Prisoners were often tortured in the yard before they were thrown into solitary confinement. The cellblock is oppressive and the bare cells gave no comfort to the prisoners, some were converted into tiny standing cells designed to stop the men sitting or lying down. Some cells have exhibits depicting the terrible conditions suffered by the inmates. Cells to the left of the main entrance were used to imprison errant SS soldiers.

After the cellblock, return to the front of the Administration Building and cross the parade ground to visit the two Barrack Blocks; the right hand block has original fittings. The wooden three tier bunk beds and lockers had to be kept clean and tidy to avoid punishment. The washroom and toilet area are extremely primitive. Around fifty prisoners were supposed to live in each room but towards the end of the war many more were crammed into the blocks.

Above: The prisoners were kept in small bare cells in this block.

Right: Cell door in the Punishment Block.

Above: The Protestant Memorial.

Above: The Catholic Memorial.

Below: The Jewish Memorial.

Above: The Russian Memorial.

Left: Victims would have stripped here before entering the gas chamber.

Right: The Gas Chamber.

Below: The crematoria were kept busy until coal stocks ran low.

The memorial to the unknown prisoner.

Follow the wide road down the centre of the camp, passing between the two lines of poplar trees. The compound is now a huge gravel area with kerbstones and numbered stones marking the outline of each block. These blocks were built in 1936 and the area was crammed with prisoners working under the watchful eye of their capos.

The memorials stand in a row at the north end of the camp. The door in the guard tower behind the Catholic Chapel leads into the Carmelite convent.

The crematorium is across a small bridge at the northwest corner of the camp. A number of memorials, including one for the unknown prisoner and another to commemorate Russian prisoners are in the area. The large brick built Barrack X with its menacing chimney stands in the centre of a clearing. A plaque marks the spot where prisoners were executed on a gallows near the south end of the building and a shooting range where prisoners were executed is to the north. Four women of the British Special Operations Executive (SOE) were executed here on 2 September 1944 (Mrs Yolande Beekman, Miss Madeleine Damerment, Miss Noorunisa Inayat Khan and Mrs Elaine Plewman).

The ashes of thousands of unknown victims were buried behind the crematorium and the area is now peaceful woodland with monuments and plaques marking gravesites among the trees.

Visiting the Dachau Area

After completing your visit to the camp return to your car and turn left out of the car park. The plantation was just beyond the end of the camp wall, on Hans Böckler Strasse to the right.

The Plantation

Hundreds of prisoners worked under severe conditions at the medicinal herb garden. Inmates were often drowned in the pond and Jewish prisoners were singled out for beatings and attacks by the guards' dogs. A few managed to get work in the greenhouses and sheds where there was a better chance of survival but at the end of each shift the exhausted prisoners returned to the main camp pushing barrows filled with the dead and dying.

Continue north past the Plantation and after half a mile turn right at the T-junction onto Freisingerstrasse. A sign indicates the entrance to the site of the SS Firing Range after 300m. Turn left into the driveway and pass through the gates into a small car park. The secluded firing range is through the trees to the north.

The Plantation Building.

Herbertshausen SS Firing Range

In 1941 and 1942 thousands of captured Russian soldiers were brought to Dachau and those suspected of being Communist Commissars were executed at the firing range, a violation of the Geneva Convention. Russia had refused to sign the Convention so Hitler felt justified in ordering their execution.

The soldiers were brought here in groups of between 50 and 120 men where they were stripped and held in the eastern shooting lane. Guards handcuffed the men, a handful at a time, to wooden posts in the western lane. They were shot while the rest stood only yards away. Over 4,000 were executed.

The Herbertshausen SS Firing Range where 4,000 Soviet prisoners were executed.

Return to the main road and turn right. After passing under a railway bridge, turn right into the first narrow road; there is a car park in the trees. Leitenberg Cemetery is hidden at the top of the hill; follow one of the paths leading to the summit 300m to the west.

Leitenberg Cemetery

After October 1944 Dachau crematorium was rarely used due to a coal shortage. Bodies were buried in *KZ-Friedhof auf der Leiten* (Leiten Concentration Camp Cemetery) on this isolated hill. The Americans discovered the cemetery and Congressmen and film makers watched as 45th Division's bulldozers began digging mass graves on 13 May.

Farm wagons stacked high with corpses were hauled through the town for everyone to see and some townsfolk were ordered to help bury the 2,400 bodies. General Robert Frederick wanted the people of Dachau to remember what had happened so close to their homes.

Now over 7,400 men and women are buried in the woods, the majority unknown. Two steep paths lead up to the top of the hill, one to the Italian Memorial and the other to the Memorial Hall. There are two monuments by the main gate, one German, the other Polish; a Jewish memorial stands in the centre of the cemetery alongside a memorial wall.

Return to your car and turn right onto the main road heading into Dachau. Continue straight on into the town and across a railway level crossing. Turn right at the traffic lights onto Krankenhausstrasse, half a mile beyond the crossing, to visit the Waldfriedhof; there is a small car park by the cemetery gates.

This memorial remembers Polish prisoners buried at Leitenberg Cemetery.

The Jewish Memorial stands next to the wall of remembrance.

Waldfriedhof

Waldfriedhof was opened during World War II and much of the work being carried out by prisoners. Jewish prisoners who died on the death march from Flossenbürg camp are buried near the entrance. Over 1,200 ex-prisoners who died of typhus and malnutrition after the liberation were also buried here. An Austrian memorial was erected in 1950 and a Jewish memorial was added in 1964.

Turn around and return along Krankenhausstrasse, heading straight on at the crossroads into Augsburgerstrasse. Stop near the church and the Rathaus.

The Town Uprising

As the Allies closed in, a few prisoners prepared to make a stand against their guards and while Arthur Haulot, Albert Guérisse (known as Patrick O'Leary when he helped Allied pilots to escape), Kazimierz Maliszewski, Edmond Michelet and Albanian Ali Kuci organised resistance in the infirmary, while Communist prisoners rallied around Oskar Müller.

Georg Scherer, an early prisoner, organised a revolt in the town with fifteen escaped prisoners and members of the *Volkssturm* on 28 April. The group occupied the Town Hall where they battled with the SS for several hours. Seven resistance fighters were killed and the SS left six of the bodies in front of the town bank as a warning (they were buried in the Waldfriedhof). Although the revolt had been suppressed, it had panicked the Germans and many left

The art gallery stands in Resistance Square.

The memorial remembers six of the men killed during the uprising.

195

The GIs were appalled by what they found in the Death Train. As a result many surrendering and captured SS guards were being shot out of hand.

later that night, abandoning their plans to evacuate the camp.

The market square was named 'Widerstandsplatz' (Resistance Square) in November 1946 and a commemorative plaque naming six of those killed in the uprising can be found on the wall of the art gallery where their bodies were left.

Continue through the square along Konrad-Adenauer Strasse, straight on at the traffic lights and turn right onto Erich-Ollenhauer Strasse beyond the level crossing. After 1/4 mile turn left into Theodor Heuss Strasse and immediately bear right at John F Kennedy Platz into Strasse der KZ-Opfer. The Death Train was found close to the square.

The Death Train

The first signs that all was not well at Dachau as American troops closed in on 29 April 1945 came to the attention of 45th Division's men near the southwest corner of the camp. They found a train parked on a siding with around twenty wagons filled with bodies; it was soon known as the Death Train. Before long the Americans were taking their revenge on the SS guards rounded up in the Dachau barracks. Hans Merbach was later convicted and executed on 14 January 1949.

The SS Barrack blocks line the road and the large administration building is to the left; the Commandant's Building is at the end. Take the right hand fork into Pater-Roth Strasse and follow it past the concentration camp car park to complete your circuit of the town.

Guards' Barracks line SS Road.

Guards were trained in the huge administration building.

197

A close-up of the memorial in front of the building; skeleton-like figures hang from the electric fence.

קיינמאָל מער
PLUS JAMAIS
NEVER AGAIN
NIE WIEDER
НИКОГДА БОЛЬШЕ

Never Again; the simple message to future generations.

Chapter Ten

MUNICH

As THE HORRIFYING TRUTH AT DACHAU CAMP was being uncovered on 29 April, XV Corps was closing in on Munich from all sides. General Haislip's priority was to seal off the city and then seize bridges across the River Isar to the east to stop the German troops fleeing into the Alps.

To the west, 3rd Division was racing down the roads either side of the Augsburg autobahn having left 15th Regiment behind to garrison the city. General O'Daniel had ordered every available vehicle forward so that his two Task Forces could circle around the southern outskirts of Munich and reach the Isar. Task Force Osgard had 30th Regiment's 2nd Battalion leading and

The noose tightens on Munich as American troops throw a cordon around the city.

The local population watched in silence as American tanks rolled past.

Colonel Lionel McGarr and Lieutenant-Colonel James Osgard had gone ahead and found that the bridge over the River Amper was still standing. They ordered the Task Force to drive across at full speed and Captain Robert Fleet's Company F crossed first, braving heavy fire to reach the German engineers as they put the finishing touches to their explosives. Fleet's men won the race and crossed before they could be detonated but they had to fight for their lives to

hold the slender bridgehead on the far bank while the rest of 3rd Division crossed. The autobahn turned out to be the only bridge still standing over the Amper and Company F's brave actions saved the division many hours.

Task Force Horton, based on 7th Regiment's 3rd Battalion, took over the lead on the far side of the river and moved in a huge arc around the southern outskirts of Munich in the hope of reaching the Isar before nightfall. It failed. The armoured column was brought to a standstill when it ran into fourteen 88mm guns and a large group of infantry covering Germering.

To the north of the city, 42nd Division regrouped around Dachau while 45th Division moved up to help 20th Armoured Division secure bridgeheads across the Schleissheimer Canal. 180th Regiment sent 2nd Battalion forward to help Combat Command B clear the Unter-Schleissheim railway bridge and the GIs mounted the Shermans to seize the bridge and clear the village beyond; they were across the Schleissheimer Canal by nightfall. 3rd Battalion also managed to establish a bridgehead near Ober-Schleissheim. On XV Corps' right flank 179th Regiment encountered emplaced 88mm guns covering the Nuremberg autobahn at Garching. 1st Battalion finally secured the village the following morning, clearing the left bank of the River Isar.

Directions from Dachau to the SS **Leibstandarte** *Baracks*

Head south from the concentration camp and turn left at the traffic lights after one mile, heading east along Route 471 towards Oberschleissheim. Cross the autobahn and turn right for Munich, one mile after the railway crossing. Beyond the woods is a large heath and there is a parking area to the right. The roof of a huge building can be seen on the horizon, to the right of the road; the building was the SS Leibstandarte barracks.

The Battle for the SS-Leibstandarte Barracks

By first light on 30 April XV Corps was ready to push deep into the heart of Munich but as troops infiltrated the ruins, 20th Armoured Division faced the main body of Germans gathered around the huge SS barracks in the northeast outskirts of the city. The barracks were the largest in Germany and thousands of members of the SS-*Leibstandarte Adolph Hitler* had trained there.

180th Regiment had joined Task Force 20 on the morning of 30 April for the attack and the GIs faced a formidable task. Over 700 SS soldiers were waiting in a network of trenches and bunkers covering the open ground in front of the barracks and anti-tank ditches and barbed wire had been prepared to funnel the American troops into minefields. The huge six-storey barracks, (measuring 300 metres square) stood at the far end of the open heath surrounded by a three-metre high concrete wall and another 800 SS troops had been working around the clock to turn the building into a fortress; at least ten 88mm guns and several 20mm flak guns formed the backbone of the defence. At the nearby anti-tank school more soldiers were waiting for the attack to begin. It was going to be the SS-*Leibstandarte*'s final stand, a fight to the death for the Führer.

The attack was supposed to begin after a short bombardment but a breakdown in communications delayed the infantry and 20th Tank Battalion advanced alone towards the barracks. As the American tanks lurched forwards across the open field, the area erupted as the Germans opened fire from their camouflaged positions. Company D's M5 Stuarts weaved towards the anti-tank barracks and the Germans did not score their first hit until the tanks were near the perimeter wall. Captain Heiler was killed as he went to rescue a crew member from a blazing tank and a second Stuart exploded in a sheet of flame when an 88 shell ripped through its thin armour. Across the road three Shermans were hit as they crawled towards the barracks, leaving 20th Tank Battalion no option but to withdraw and reorganise.

Over two hours passed before a second attack was made with the infantry in support and Colonel Duvall's men huddled behind Company A's tanks as they rumbled forward, drawing fire from every window in the barracks. Yet again the 88s proved to be deadly and after the third Sherman burst into flames, the Company commander recalled the survivors.

General Ward's requests for air strikes were refused due to the overcast skies so Colonel Lewis Ham, the divisional artillery commander, was ordered to renew the bombardment. 975th Field Artillery Battalion's huge 155mm howitzers began tearing huge holes in the barracks and 413th Armoured Field Artillery Battalion's 105mm howitzers shelled the fields in front while the tanks and infantry regrouped. The barrage achieved little. The shells were unable to penetrate the bunkers and the SS opened fire as soon as the third attack began.

The huge SS Barracks, scene of the last stand in the Munich area. Inset: Hitler inspects a soldier's locker in the barracks.

Many Germans waited until Colonel Carns' tanks and halftracks had passed by before emerging to fire on their backs. Colonel Duvall's infantry following on foot turned to engage them and furious hand-to-hand fighting followed. Some SS troopers elected to stay hidden, looking for an opportunity to surface when all the Americans had passed and Colonel Carns had to call up the engineers' tank dozers to watch over the largest bunkers.

The fighting was ferocious and usually no mercy was shown, even to the wounded. When one crew stopped to accept the surrender of a bunker, an SS soldier disabled the tank with his *panzerfaust*, ignoring his comrades' white flag. In a rare display of compassion the Germans evacuated the seriously wounded commander as others climbed into the tank and turned the gun on the advancing American soldiers. The episode came to an end when 88s near the barracks finished off the stricken tank unaware that it had been captured.

Despite the heavy fighting, the German trenches and bunkers were cleared one by one and as the GIs poured into the barracks, the battle continued across the parade ground and into the buildings. Many SS soldiers fought to the death while others slipped away into the city in the hope of continuing the fight. By nightfall it was all over; the ruins of the SS *Leibstandarte* Barracks were in American hands. Ironically Adolf Hitler committed suicide in his bunker below the streets of Berlin on the same day that his bodyguard fought their last battle.

The Battle for Munich

While the battle for the barracks raged and the rest of XV Corps increased its grip on Munich, Troop D of the 33rd Cavalry had slipped through the German lines heading for three important buildings. One platoon had to find Munich Radio studios near the railway station on the west side of the city while a second needed to cross the River Isar to capture the radio transmitter at Ismaning. Sixth Army Group wanted to use the facilities to broadcast messages, (in particular the news of Hitler's suicide) to the German Armed Forces and civilians. The third target was the Munich newspaper office (home of the *Volkischer Beobachter*) in the southeast corner of the city. The presses would be used to print posters and newsletters for distribution across southern Germany.

3rd Platoon's mission started well and elements of the 106th Cavalry group joined the race into Ismaning where the transmitter was captured intact, along with many of the staff. 1st and 2nd Platoons struggled to make their way through 20th Armoured Division's backlog of vehicles waiting near Dachau and the two leaders soon decided to move off the main roads at the start of a

News of Hitler's death was quickly flashed around the world.

reckless drive through the streets past snipers and roadblocks. The inmates of a slave labour camp overwhelmed the small group of jeeps when the two platoon sergeants stopped to check directions and it took some time to explain that the main force was still down the road. A British prisoner joined the American Task Force as a guide and as they headed deeper into the city, a member of the German underground led the GIs towards their objectives on a bicycle as civilians showered them with flowers and gifts. The column also liberated 150 American POWs and they joined the group. The strange procession eventually captured both their targets and before long the American Forces Network was broadcasting from the radio station.

Meanwhile, the rest of XV Corps had to fight their way into the city and 157th Regiment spent the day seizing bridgeheads across the Schleissheimer Canal to the west. 2nd Battalion spent the morning engaged at Feldmoching while 1st Battalion liberated 8,000 prisoners at one of Dachau's many sub camps. On the east flank 179th Regiment had finally cleared Garching and moved into Munich's suburbs, securing bridges across the River Isar.

In 42nd Division's sector, west of Dachau, 242nd Regiment led, capturing 100 planes and over 1,500 *Luftwaffe* personnel at an airstrip on the outskirts of the city. There was little resistance as they entered the suburbs and the streets were soon filled with freed prisoners and civilians as the advance turned into a victory parade. As the crowds became restless and began looting warehouses, Lieutenant-Colonel George Fricke regained control by posting sentries and putting many civilians to work clearing rubble from the streets.

Koenigsplatz, the site of Hitler's offices and the headquarters of the Nazi Party, were taken by 242nd Regiment and many of Fricke's men took the opportunity to visit the palatial buildings. General Collins eventually set up his headquarters in the nearby *Rathaus* (town hall) as his staff began to take control of the city.

To the south 3rd Division was still trying to reach the River Isar and 7th Regiment finally cleared Germering. 1st Battalion found a large group of SS troops and Hitler Youth in Pullach and they destroyed the bridge before the GIs could cross. With the way east blocked, General O'Daniel ordered both of his regiments to turn north into Munich. Once again, as soon as his men had passed the ring of anti-aircraft guns covering the outskirts, they were able to move quickly into the heart of the city, finding a mixed reaction from the citizens. Many GIs were showered with flowers while men and civilians pointed out where soldiers were hiding in some streets, while rearguards fired upon them in others. Late in the afternoon General O'Daniel rode into the centre of the city, planning to arrange a formal surrender with the Nazi commanders. He was disappointed to discover that they had already fled, leaving behind three junior officials to meet the Americans.

The last pockets of resistance were cleared on 1 May, leaving XV Corps with a huge logistical headache. Munich usually had a population of around

Armoured columns pushed quickly into the heart of the city.

In some areas the American troops were greeted with enthusiasm.

White flags hung from many buildings to indicate that German troops had already fled.

400,000 but captured soldiers, refugees and camp prisoners swelled the numbers by a further 200,000.

While the rest of XV Corps headed off at speed towards Salzburg and the Alps, 45th Division remained behind to restore order and while 157th Regiment and 191st Tank Battalion manned roadblocks in the ruins, 180th Regiment set up a number of prisoner of war camps; its staff would eventually process over 125,000 German soldiers. The divisional headquarters was also

Members of the Hitler Youth were quickly rounded up.

busy on 3 May when the Commanding General of the *9th Hungarian Division* surrendered his staff and 7,400 men to General Frederick; they were assembled in a makeshift camp on the city's airport and put under guard. One Battalion of 179th Regiment was given the gruesome task of clearing up Dachau concentration camp while the rest of 179th Regiment was held on stand-by ready to quell any rioting.

The priority was to install a military government and restore a semblance of law and order but General Frederick's staff were too busy with military problems and Major Leo Bishop, the division's G-2 officer, had to set up a new facility called Security Control Munich to deal specifically with civil affairs.

The roadblocks were kept busy to begin with as sporadic riots broke out and a curfew had to be enforced while all forms of transport were confiscated; all communications apart from the American Forces Network were also suspended. Before long the military government had Munich under control and after the chaos of the past few years the civilians welcomed the new regime and the peace it brought to their city.

Patrols and checkpoints around the city helped to maintain a strict curfew and quell riots.

Thousands of prisoners were herded into makeshift camps on the outskirts of the city.

Directions to Munich Railway Station (Bahnhof)

Head south past the SS Barracks. The buildings are now flats and although fascia panels cover the concrete walls the huge symmetrical structure and its high concrete wall are still menacing.

Continue along Route 13 through the suburbs for 2 miles, then turn left onto the ring road (Schenkendorfstrasse) and follow the dual carriageway through tunnels. It crosses the River Isar after two miles. Carry straight on at Effnerplatz (a roundabout in 2005, soon to be a tunnel) and turn right at the next traffic lights into Denningerstrasse. Take the first left into Delphstrasse (known as Wasserburgerstrasse in the 1930s) and head south through the sleepy suburb; Eva Braun's home, Number 12, is on the left after 400m, partially hidden behind a high wall. (The house is now a private residence; please respect the owner's privacy.)

Continue to the end of Delphstrasse, turning left into Röntgenstrasse at the end. Take the right fork after 200m and go straight across Mühlbaurstrasse into Brucknerstrasse. Turn right on to the main street Prinzregenstrasse after 200m and enter Prinzregentenplatz after 300m. Hitler's apartment was on the left as you enter the square, on the second floor of Number 16 (the ground floor is now a police station).

Carry straight on through the square, heading west, and after 1/2 mile the road winds its way down to the River Isar past a tall obelisk topped with the huge golden Angel of Peace (Friedensengel). Cross the river and continue straight on into the tunnel after 1/2 mile. Continue straight on along the inner ring road at the far end of the tunnel through Maximilians-platz and turn right at Karlz-platz (one of the old city gates is to the left) into Bayerstrasse. The railway station is after 300m. Find a parking space in one of the many car parks in the area and walk back to the railway station to start the walking tour of the city.

A Walking Tour of Munich Centre

The railway station has a tourist information shop, where it is possible to buy maps, tourist guides and souvenirs from, by the main entrance on the east side. Heading east from the shop, follow Bayerstrasse from the southeast corner of Bahnhofplatz for 300m to Karlsplatz, a large roundabout; head straight on via the underpass towards Karl Tor (one of the medieval town gates) at the far

ee
ap
n
age
22

Hoffmann discusses a matter with his friend.

Hitler and Heinrich Hoffmann rented number 12 Delphstrasse (Wasserburgerstrasse at the time) for Eva Braun and her younger sister Gretl. The two young ladies worked at Hoffmann's photographic studio in the centre of Munich and Eva became Hitler's mistress in 1932. Hoffmann had been the Nazi Party's photographer since the early days and his business became extremely lucrative as the Party rose to power, making large sums of money from picture albums of Hitler. Eva Braun became Hitler's constant companion but she did not get her final wish until 30 April 1945 when the pair married in the Führer's bunker beneath the streets of Berlin; they committed suicide the following day as the Russians closed in.

Eva Braun's flat in Munich's suburbs.

211

Geli Raubal   Eva Braun

Hitler's Munich flat during his rise to power.

Hitler obtained the luxury flat in 1929 and his sister, Mrs Raubal, joined him as housekeeper, bringing her two daughters with her. Geli Raubal had been Hitler's companion for some time and Nazi leaders frowned on the relationship as talk spread that they were lovers. Tensions in the relationship increased as Hitler's status grew and Geli was accused of having an affair with his chauffeur. She was found dead in the flat in September 1931 and Hitler fell into a deep depression as rumours spread throughout the Nazi hierarchy. Had he shot her during an argument or had she been murdered on Heinrich Himmler's orders? The official version was suicide.

side of the square. Pass beneath the gate and walk along Neuhauser Strasse, a pedestrian precinct filled with shops and restaurants. St Michael's Church and the former Jesuit College are to the left after 250m; the German Hunting Museum is in the Augustine Church next door. Continue east into Marienplatz, noting the twin towers of the Dom with their round cupolas to the left. The spectacular Town Hall (Rathaus), with its neo Gothic façade, tower and Glockenspiel (an array of figures that perform on the hour) stands on the north side of the square.

Walk straight across the square, passing the Old Town Hall (Alte Rathaus) and enter the street called Tal. Continue past Heiliggeist Church and after 250m is a furniture shop with the address Tal 38. Sterneckerbräu Brewery became the first headquarters of the NSDAP in February 1920 and Hitler had his first office in the building. He took command of the NSDAP here in January 1921 and planned his early speeches for meetings in the nearby Hofbräuhaus. New offices had to be found in Schellingstrasse after he was released from Landsberg Prison in December 1924. The Nazis turned the building into a shrine when they seized power.

Turn round and retrace your steps

The NSDAP's first headquarters.

The magnificent Town Hall.

along Tal, taking the first right into Hochbrucken after 100m. Take the second left into Brauhausstrasse after 150m and the entrance to the Hofbräuhaus Brewery and tavern is to the right in Am Platz.

The building has changed little over the years and on 24 February 1920 the NSDAP held its first mass meeting in the first floor Festsaal. Hitler had spoken at smaller meetings before but his announcement of the Party's Twenty-Five Points, the cornerstone of Nazi beliefs, grabbed the attention of the large crowd.

Continue past the front of the building and after 150m turn left into Maximillianstrasse, heading west to Max Joseph Platz and a large statue of the King. The National Theatre, home of the Bavarian State Opera, and the Old Residency Theatre occupy two sides of the square and the Residenz, the royal residence for the Bavarian rulers, fills the north side of the square. The huge complex now has seven courtyards, the Hercules Hall, the Museum and the Treasury.

Cross the square to the north corner and walk down Residenzstrasse, with the Residenz to your right. The street opens into Odeonplatz after 200m and the

History of Munich (München)

The capital of Bavaria began in the early Middle Ages as a small religious settlement on the banks of the Isar. Henry the Lion built a new ford in 1158 so he could tax traders travelling between the Alps and Augsburg. Twenty years later Emperor Frederick I gave control of Bavaria to Count Otto von Wittelsbach and his family remained in power until the end of the First World War. Fortifications were added and after 1255 successive rulers lived in the Residency, raising Munich to city status. Trouble flared in the 17th Century as the city formed the centre for Maximillian I's Catholic League during the Thirty Years' War and the Swedish Protestant King attacked it. Further wars and plagues continued to trouble the inhabitants but Munich survived to emerge as the capital of Bavaria when it was granted a monarchy by Napoleon in 1806. Over the years that followed both King Ludwig I and King Max II turned Munich into an architectural delight but the end of the First World War was the start of turbulent times for the city. It was the scene of violent clashes between National Socialist supporters and Communists, culminating in the Putsch in 1923 where the police made a stand in Odenplatz, killing several activists. Hitler was later arrested and imprisoned in Landsberg prison. He returned to the city in 1925 and the reformed Nazi Party began its steady growth to power, basing its headquarters in the city; eventually a large number of buildings around Königsplatz formed the organisation's seat of power.

The Allied bombings towards the end of the Second World War devastated Munich but many of the architectural monuments have been restored and the city is now a delight to walk around.

The Hofbrauhaus.

The Dom's twin towers
are a feature of the
Munich skyline.

*Temple of Fame (Feldherrnhalle) is to the left where the
1923 Putsch came to an end.*

*Walk across Odeonplatz, with the impressive
Theatiner Church to your left, and turn left into
Briennerstrasse by the statue of Ludwig I. Head west for
300m (passing Ludwig-Ferdinand's palace and
Maximillian's statue) to a memorial marking the end of
National Socialism. Continue straight ahead on
Briennerstrasse and Türkenstrasse is to the right after
150m. The Munich Police had its headquarters in this
street. Heinrich Himmler was head of the Munich Police
immediately after the Nazis' takeover in March 1933,
and along with Reinhard Heydrich, head of the Party's
Security Services (SD) he had hundreds of political
opponents brought to the building for questioning before
they were sent to Dachau concentration camp.*

*Continue straight on to Karolinenplatz with its tall
obelisk. The Nazi Party's Legal offices were to the right as
you enter the square, at the end of Max-Joseph Strasse.
The Nazis' Supreme Court occupied the building to the
right front, and their Audit and Accounts Offices were to the left front. Follow
Barerstrasse, the left hand exit from the square and pass the Nazi Organisation's
Leadership offices and Ernst Rohm's headquarters for the SA (Sturmabteilung) or
Brownshirts, on the right. The Hitler Youth Headquarters were on the left, alongside
Heinrich Hoffmann's photographic studio where Eva Braun worked.*

*After 200m turn right into Karlstrasse; the SS headquarters and Party's post
office occupied the buildings on the corners. Heading west, the buildings on the right
were NSDAP offices, including the Hitler Youth, the Students Association, the Press
Office, the Foreign Press Office and the all important Party Propaganda office where*

The Munich Putsch

On the evening of 8 November 1923 Hitler, Göring and Field Marshall Erich Ludendorff forcefully entered a government meeting in the Bürgerbräukeller armed with guns. They announced to the 3,000 strong crowds that a revolution had broken out and took the gathered leaders prisoner and forced them to support the coup. Although some SA stormtroopers had seized the police and Army headquarters, others failed to take their objectives and the revolt quickly descended into chaos. The three leaders were released and immediately called for help as the putschists argued over what to do next.

Around noon the following day Hitler, Göring and Ludendorff led around 2,000 supporters through the streets (passing through Isar Tor, along Tal to the Town Hall, where they turned north along Residenzstrasse towards Odeonplatz). Police were waiting by the Feldherrnhalle and after a few shots were fired in the standoff, a fierce gun battle followed. Fourteen putschists and four police were killed; Göring was shot in the leg while Hitler suffered injuries when he fell to the ground. The Putsch was over and the NSDAP leaders were quickly rounded up. Several, including Hitler, were imprisoned in Landsberg Prison.

The site became a memorial when the Nazis returned to power and each anniversary the Putsch leaders led a procession through the streets to honour those killed and lay wreaths by new memorials on the Feldherrnhalle. Odeonplatz also became an important arena for parades.

Hitler and Ludendorff who led the Putsch.

The Nazi Old Guard follow the route of the Putsch along Tal.

Hitler lays a wreath at the martyrs' memorial.
Left: The same location today; the site of the plaque can still be seen on the wall.

Joseph Goebbels' organisation operated from.

Turn right into Meiserstrasse after 200m. Many officials lived in the block to the right, where there were apartments, meeting rooms and an independent power plant to provide heating and light for the Party Buildings. The offices of the Party's big three were to the left; the Party Treasurer, Martin Bormann, Head of the Four Year Plan, Hermann Goering, and the Führer's Deputy, Rudolf Hess.

Königsplatz is to the left after 200m. The crossroads at the east end of the square were the symbolic centre of the Nazi Party's organisation. Their headquarters were moved to the Brown house in January 1931 and the building once stood

Odeonplatz during the ceremony to relocate the bodies of the martyrs to Königsplatz.

on the left hand side of Brienstrasse, to the right. The building was badly damaged by Allied bombing and it was later torn down; the foundations have recently been excavated. The Papal Nuncio occupied the building opposite. Immediately north and south of the crossroads are two areas of trees and undergrowth barely concealing steps. These were the Temples of Honour (Ehrentempeln), two pantheons built to house the sarcophagi of the men killed in the putsch. The US Army demolished the two temples in 1947.

Two large identical buildings flank the Temples of Honour. To the south was the NSDAP's Administration Building, the

The Temple of Fame.

Verwaltungsbau, where the operations of all the departments were coordinated. To the north was Hitler's office building, the Führerbau, where the Munich Agreement ceding the German-speaking Sudetenland of Czechoslovakia was signed in September 1938. After the German Army had mobilised on the Czech border, the British Prime Minister, Neville Chamberlain visited Hitler twice (the first time at

A guard of honour prepares to lay wreaths at one of the Temples of Honour.

The NSDAP's hierarchy occupied many of the buildings along Karlstrasse.

Berchtesgaden) to try and appease him. Hitler refused and at a third meeting at the Führerbau an agreement was signed handing over the Sudetenland. The following are some of the leading personalities who were present. Germany: Adolf Hitler, Joachim von Ribbentrop, Hermann Göring, Heinrich Himmler, Rudolf Hess, and General Wilhelm Keitel (Chief of Staff). Italy: Benito Mussolini. Great Britain: Neville Chamberlain and his ambassador. France: The French Premier, Edouard Daladier, and his ambassador.

Neville Chamberlain returned to England and declared that the papers assured

From left to right, the offices of Bormann, Goering and Hess.

The Führerbrau where the Munich Agreement was signed.

'peace in our time'. He was sadly wrong. German troops marched into the rest of Czechoslovakia in March 1939 and six months later, Europe was at war.

Although the Americans considered demolishing the Nazi buildings there was an acute lack of office space after the war and Hitler's offices were turned into an Information Centre for US Armed Forces and renamed Amerika Haus; the building is now a music school. Opposite is Königsplatz (King's Square) built in the reign of King Ludwig. A triumphal arch and two classical buildings, the Collection of Antiquities Building (Staatsgalerie) and the Glypothek (Art Gallery), surround the

Looking back across Königsplatz towards the Führer's office and one of the Temples of Honour during one of the parades.

One of the many ceremonies held in the square.

Königsplatz's triumphal arch.

The Antiquities building.

The Art Gallery.

square. The original Art Gallery burned down in 1931 and a new, Third Reich style, House of German Art (Haus der Deutschen Kunst) was opened on the site in July 1937. The area was paved over for parades during the Nazi era and in May 1933 thousands of books were burned in the square during Goebbels propaganda campaign against banned literature; the grassed areas have been reinstated.

Retrace your steps, heading south along Meiserstrasse and turn left into Sophienstrasse after 350m. The street joins Luissenstrasse after 250m; turn left and the railway station (your start point) is to the right after 250m.

Thousands of books written by authors considered to be enemies to National Socialism were burned in Königsplatz in May 1933.

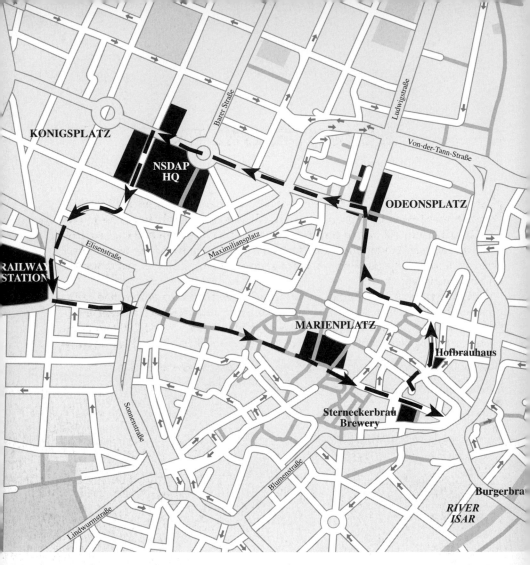

Walking tour around Münich.

The 1923 Putsch started at the Bürgerbräukeller, crossed the River Isar at Ludwigsbrücke and followed Tal to Marienplatz. Hitler's supporters then turned right and headed north until they were stopped in Odensplatz.

Chapter Eleven

BERCHTESGADEN

S NOW FELL ACROSS BAVARIA as 3rd Division prepared for the final
advance towards Salzburg. The end of the war was only hours away but
the division still had to complete one final task; the men had to head east
towards Salzburg to stop die-hard Nazis fleeing into the Alps. The two leading
Regiments were organised into fast moving task forces, with the men mounted
on all kinds of vehicle.

15th Regiment's 2nd Battalion formed Task Force Ware and it had soon
crossed the River Isar south of Munich, meeting hundreds of surrendering
German soldiers as it headed east towards Holzkirchen; over 1,400 had been
collected by nightfall. 30th Regiment's 3rd Battalion had the task of clearing

Thousands of prisoners gather around planes on an abandoned airfield.

The Allied Air Forces had driven the Luftwaffe into hiding and these GIs have discovered an abandoned Me 262 Jet Fighter in the undergrowth by the side of an autobahn.

the roads north of the Salzburg autobahn and Task Force Chaney found three hundred planes, many with their engines running, on Neubiberg airport south of Munich. As patrols secured the perimeter and rounded up the *Luftwaffe* personnel, the rest of the column headed east along the autobahn. Lieutenant-Colonel Christopher Chaney wanted to reach Rosenheim, over thirty miles to the southeast, in the shortest time possible. His objective was to secure bridges over the River Inn, the last major river before Salzburg, before the German engineers destroyed them.

Intelligence reports suggested that four battalions held Rosenheim but Company I managed to infiltrate the outskirts of the town and reach the river before they were spotted. The guards at two secondary bridges were overpowered before they could detonate the explosives. Two platoons of Company L followed and found a rearguard waiting at the main highway bridge. As the GIs sprinted across the bridge, dodging mines as they ran, Lieutenant Emil Byke clambered under the deck and cut the burning fuse moments before the demolition charges blew up the bridge.

With the crossings secure, Company I had to turn their attentions to clearing Rosenheim. Rather than taking the town by force, Lieutenant Mehuron arranged a meeting with the German commander and convinced him that a huge force of infantry and tanks was about to attack. The ruse worked and Company I was soon busy organising over 1,600 prisoners.

Beyond Rosenheim, Task Force Chaney headed east along the autobahn as the GIs marvelled at the sight of the huge inland lake, the Chiemsee, and the foothills of the Alps. To view such natural beauty after the horrors of the past few weeks was a surreal experience. Beyond the lake, the task force headed into Traunstein where it was halted as 20th Armoured Division and a French Division passed through heading for Salzburg, creating a traffic jam on the only remaining bridge in the town.

As the two Task Forces reorganised, 7th Regiment took over the advance along the autobahn, bypassing a destroyed bridge near Obersee, and 3rd Battalion fought its last battle in the town of Siegsdorf. 2nd Battalion reached the Austrian border on 3 May, finding all three bridges across the Saalach River destroyed, and it was forced to make one last assault crossing later that night. To the north, 3rd Division's Assistant Divisional Commander, Brigadier-General Robert Young, led the reconnaissance vehicles of 106th Cavalry Group into Salzburg where he accepted the surrender of the city from the garrison

German soldiers march into captivity as 3rd Division heads towards the Alps.

There was no time to enjoy the Alpine scenery as Seventh Army raced to cut off the passes into the 'National Redoubt'.

commander and local dignitaries.

By now news of Hitler's death on 30 April had spread and 3rd Division was overwhelmed with prisoners as complete units surrendered (one battalion surrendered to a solitary GI who had become separated from the rest of his company). One battalion took over 3,000 prisoners including three Generals.

Directions from Munich to Winkl

Starting from Münich Railway Station follow Arnulfstrasse, running parallel with the north side of the station. After 1½ miles turn left onto Lanshuterstrasse, the ring road, and head south over the railway sidings and through a tunnel. At the junction with Autobahn 95 after 1½ miles, continue to follow the ring road (Route 2R) and signs for Salzburg; it turns into Autobahn 995 in 3½ miles.

Take the slip road at junction 6 for Autobahn 8 after 7 miles, heading for Salzburg. The foothills of the Alps begin to appear to the right, getting higher and higher as you head towards the Austrian border. After 45 miles the large inland lake called Chiemsee is to the left of the road and the autobahn begins to climb through the foothills as it continues east. After another 29 miles exit at junction 115, signposted for Bad Reichenhall, turning right at the end of the slip road and again right at the roundabout. In Bad Reichenhall turn right onto the slip road signposted for Berchtesgaden and follow the road south as it heads into the mountains. Winkl is after 5 miles.

The Surrender of Berchtesgaden

Berchtesgaden was supposed to have been occupied by the 101st Airborne Division but General O'Daniel was determined that his men would have the honour of seizing the town and Hitler's complex on Obersalzberg. Blown bridges had delayed 506th Parachute Regiment as it approached from the west along the picturesque Alpenstrasse so Colonel Robert Sink decided to follow 3rd Division along the autobahn. General O'Daniel personally halted the airborne troops at the only bridge across the River Saalbach; (he also stopped the 2nd French Armoured Division from crossing after a heated argument with General Le Clark). O'Daniel then ordered Colonel Heintges to send a Task Force towards Berchtesgaden and 7th Regiment's 1st Battalion was chosen to lead the way. After taking 3,000 prisoners in Bad Reichenhall it headed towards Bischofswiesen while 3rd Battalion approached Berchtesgaden from the northeast.

As the American columns moved along the alpine passes, Theodor Jacob, the Berchtesgaden District Commissioner, was determined to make sure that his townspeople did not suffer. District leader Stredele, a fanatic Nazi, was determined to fight but the Obersalzberg's SS commander, Bernhard Frank,

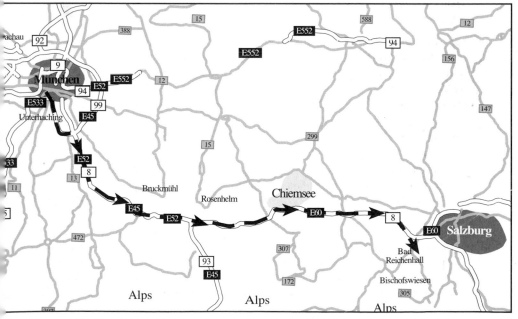

The road to the Alps.

Many Germans realised that the war was over but groups of SS soldiers continued to fight on in the mountain villages.

and the head of the staff, *Ingenieur* Grethlein, both gave assurances that their men were abandoning Hitler's mountain complex and withdrawing into the mountains. Jacob was then able to disband the town's *Volkssturm* and then headed north to greet the advancing American troops.

He met an armoured column of 30th Infantry Regiment at the tiny hamlet of Winkl, north of Bischofswiesen, and declared Berchtesgaden an open town. Lieutenant-Colonel Kenneth Wallace insisted that the formal surrender took place in the centre of the town and Jacob led the column of tanks and lorries through the mountains and into the heart of Berchtesgaden. He formally surrendered the community outside the town hall (Rathaus). General O'Daniel eventually let the paratroopers and the French troops across the river when Colonel Heingtes confirmed that his men had reached the Berghof on Obersalzberg.

Directions from Winkl to Stanggass

2½ miles beyond Winkl, turn left for Berchtesgaden and pass through Stanggass.

Stanggass

Hitler decided to build a government complex in Stanggass as he spent more and more time at the Berghof. A Chancellery building (Reichskanzlei) and security buildings were built in 1936 to serve as a second seat of government and a diplomatic centre. *Generalfeldmarschall* Wilhelm Keitel, Chief of Staff of the Armed Forces, and *Generaloberst* Alfred Jodl, Chief of the Operations Staff, also had houses in the village. A large hospital (Dietrich-Eckart-Krankenhaus) was built on the slopes above Stanggass in 1940.

Berchtesgaden

Rich salt deposits in the mountains surrounding Berchtesgaden made it an important trading centre in the Middle Ages. It was ceded to Bavaria in 1810 and immediately became popular with the Royal Family and they built a large hunting lodge in the town. Towards the end of the 19th Century tourists began

Theodor Jacob met Colonel Wallace's men at Winkl, several miles north of Berchtesgaden

Tense moments as 3rd Division moves towards Berchtesgaden; would the Germans make a stand around Hitler's Alpine retreat or not?

to visit the area to enjoy the mountains and take in the alpine air but in 1923 one visitor changed Berchtesgaden's place in history for ever; that visitor was Adolf Hitler.

Directions from Stanggass to Berchtesgaden

Just beyond Stanggass, the road bends sharply to the left by the Berchtesgaden sign and heads down to a small roundabout; head straight on for the centre of the town.

Before the roundabout is the imposing Berchtesgadener Hof Hotel, now abandoned, to the right. The NSDAP bought the Grand Hotel Auguste Victoria in 1936 and redesigned it in the style of the times for senior Nazi officials,

Berchtesgadener Hof Hotel.

statesmen and dignitaries visiting Hitler. Goebbels, Himmler, von Ribbentrop and senior generals stayed at the hotel until facilities on the Obersalzberg were built. The Duke and Duchess of Windsor (the abdicated King Edward VIII and his wife), the British Prime Minister Neville Chamberlain and retired British Prime Minister David Lloyd George also stayed here during the late 1930s. It was also Eva Braun's first home in Berchtesgaden before she moved into Hitler's Berghof and both Hitler's sister Paula and Martin Bormann's brother Alfred stayed at the hotel.

The US Army used the hotel as a headquarters following the occupation of Berchtesgaden and a number of senior German officers surrendered their commands here. *Generalfeldmarschall* Albert Kesselring, Commander in Chief of the Western Front, was found at Saalfelden, fifteen miles to the south; there he surrendered to General Maxwell Taylor, 101st Airborne Division's

Task Force Wallace rolls into Berchtesgaden.

The same corner today.

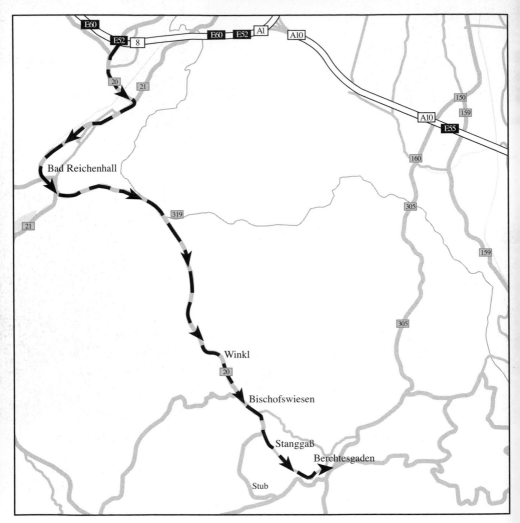

Bad Reichenhall to Berchtesgaden.

Following negotiations with American troops, German officers lead their men out of the mountains.

commanding officer. For the next fifty years the building served as United States Armed Forces Recreation Centre for troops serving in the Alps. The Army left in 1995 and it has been empty ever since.

Directions into Berchtesgaden

Follow the road into the upper part of Berchtesgaden, noting the views over the lower part of the town. There is some on-street parking along the road, and a number of small car parks if you wish to walk around the town. The tourist information centre is next to the church on the high street.

The Bergfriedhof Cemetery is next to the Tourist Information Centre. Paula Hitler, Adolf Hitler's sister, stayed on in Berchtesgaden after the war, under the name of Paula Wolf; following her death in 1960 she was buried in the local cemetery. Fritz Todt, the Nazi Armaments Minister (who died in an air crash during the war) and General Rudolf Schmundt, Hitler's Army Adjutant, are also buried here.

Upper Berchtesgaden

Cross the main street outside the centre and turn right under the archway at the far end of the market place (Marktplatz). The town war memorial is painted on the wall above the colonnade to the left. The Town Hall (Rathaus) where Theodor Jacob surrendered the town to Colonel Kenneth Wallace is just beyond the square.

Colonel Wallace accepted the surrender of the town at the Rathaus.

At over 2,700 metres high, Mount Watzmann looms over Berchtesgaden.

Lower Berchtesgaden and the railway station.

Lower Berchtesgaden

Continue down the main street and go straight on the traffic lights at the bottom of the hill. Turn immediate right into a parking area to visit Berchtesgaden railway station.

There is a short length of railway tunnel at the east end of the car park, now abandoned behind locked gates. Trains had to travel a circuitous route via Bad Reichenhall to reach Berchtesgaden and the Nazi Party planned to build a direct route to Salzburg. The line was never completed and American troops

Göring's personal train was found crammed with art treasures in this tunnel.

Berchtesgaden's huge railway station. A fleet of cars waited at the far end outside the special reception area when Hitler visited.

Robert Ley, the head of the German Labour Front (DAF) welcomes the Duke and Duchess and Windsor, (Edward and Mrs Simpson) to Berchtesgaden.

discovered a train filled with part of Hermann Göring's art collection inside the tunnel. The rest of his collection was later recovered from the tunnels beneath his house on Obersalzberg, in tunnels beneath the *Luftwaffe* headquarters in Berchtesgaden and loaded on another train in the area. They were displayed in a local hotel for a short period before the Americans took steps to return them to their rightful owners (in many cases they had died in extermination camps).

The huge station building was built in 1937 in a style and size that would suit a large town. A special reception area was built for Hitler and his guests at the far end (by the bus station) and a fleet of cars would be waiting for the Führer's entourage, ready to take them to the Berghof; other senior Nazi leaders were also taken straight to Obersalzberg. Visiting dignitaries would also be greeted and taken to the Berchtesgadener Hof Hotel where they could prepare for their visit to Hitler's mountain retreat.

Directions from Berchtesgaden to the Obersalzburg

Return to your car and turn left out of the car park, heading straight on at the traffic lights, signposted for Salzburg, and follow the river. Turn right for Obersalzberg after 1/2 mile and drive up the steep hill, taking care around the sharp bends. The visitors' car park is at the top, to the left.

Chapter Twelve

OBERSALZBERG
AND THE EAGLE'S NEST

OBERSALZBERG MOUNTAIN is two miles to the east of Berchtesgaden and 400 metres higher than the town. Small farms dotted the slopes when Mauritia (Moritz) Mayer bought Steinhaus Farm in 1877 and turned it into a guesthouse for visitors wishing to enjoy the mountain air. Pension Moritz was the first of many guesthouses and over the years that followed, the Berchtesgaden area became a popular health resort.

By the beginning of the 1920s, the number of tourists visiting the town had risen to over 36,000 a year, and many of them stayed in the farms and guesthouses on Obersalzberg. One visitor was Dietrich Eckart, a National Socialist writer and a founder member of the Munich based Nazi Party. As editor of the *Volkisher Beobachter*, Eckart's aggressive writings attracted legal action and he fled to the mountains in April 1923 to avoid a court appearance. Another Party member, Christian Weber, found him lodgings at Pension Moritz but Eckart had soon moved to Göllhäusl, a small cottage near the Platterhof Hotel, where he lived under the alias of Doctor Hoffman.

Adolf Hitler was immediately attracted to Obersalzberg.

Kampfhäusl, the tiny chalet Hitler visited to write.

Adolf Hitler had attempted to rally his supporters to take action against the Communist May Day parades but the local Reichswehr had thwarted his plans. They refused to return the Nazis' weapons and Hitler's supporters were forced to parade outside the town under police guard. Having lost face, Hitler went to Berchtesgaden under the alias of Herr Wolf where Weber led him to his old comrade and mentor. It was the start of his lifelong obsession with the Obersalzberg.

Inspired by his meeting, the NSDAP's leader returned to Munich to await his next opportunity. It came on 9 November 1923. This time the Reichswehr had given their support, but once again the *Putsch* descended into chaos, ending with a gun battle in the city streets; fourteen activists and four policemen were killed. Hitler was quickly arrested and imprisoned in Landsberg castle, forty miles west of Munich. Hitler was tried and sentenced

Hitler's view over the Platterhof Hotel.

Angela and Geli Raubal; Hitler's half sister, and niece, joined the Führer as his house-keeper.

Right: Hitler could escape the pressures of life and relax in the mountains.

Below: The mountain became a huge building site during the 1930s. This view from the roof of the Berghof shows Hotel zum Türken to the right and Bormann's house the hill.

Above: Haus Wachenfeld after Hitler had added a terrace and veranda.

Martin Bormann ruled Obersalzberg with a rod of iron.
Below: Hitler wanted his original house preserved so the building was extended in all directions.

Above: American troops pass through the Alpine style guardhouse in May 1945.

Adolf Hitlers Landhaus am Obersalzberg bei Berchtesgaden.

A postcard showing further extensions to the house.

to five years' imprisonment for treason but spent his time in relative luxury, receiving visitors as his fellow prisoners lavished praise on him. He also took the opportunity to write the first part of *Mein Kampf*, (My Struggle), putting down his beliefs on paper.

Following his release after only a year, Hitler set about rebuilding the shattered party, and by the summer of 1926 it was able to stage a large Party Rally in Weimar. Flushed with success, he returned to Obersalzberg in July and rented Kampfhäusl from the Büchner family so he could work on the second volume of *Mein Kampf*. Hitler's affection for Obersalzberg grew and his search for a permanent home ended in 1928 when he rented Haus Wachenfeld for 100 Deutchmarks a month.

With his half-sister Angela Raubal as house-keeper, Hitler settled on the mountain, returning time after time to escape the rigours of political life. Angela brought her daughters to live with her and an obsessive relationship developed between Hitler and Geli and the pair spent many hours wandering the hills together; (Geli committed suicide in Hitler's Munich flat in 1931). In 1932 Hitler put in an offer to buy the house and the owner, Mrs Winter, accepted 40,000 Goldmarks in September. The following June, the new

The new Platterhof Hotel for visitors to the Berghof.

The entrance hall.

The stately dining room.

The staff quarters and garages.

Reichchancellor took possession of his mountain retreat and set about renovating the small chalet, adding a terrace and a veranda.

Reichsleiter Martin Bormann joined the Nazi Party in 1925 after his release from jail for murder. He quickly rose through the ranks to become *Gauleiter* for Thuringia in 1928 and his skill at raising money brought him the powerful role of Party treasurer and manager of Hitler's private fortune. The workaholic Bormann shunned the limelight, preferring to spend his time catering to the Führer's whims, noting his desires and turning them into reality. One of his favourite projects was the development of the Obersalzberg complex. Bormann bought 1,000 hectares (2,400 acres) from the state and private landowners in 1935 bringing over fifty properties under Nazi rule. He bullied the owners into leaving over the next four years, threatening some with imprisonment in Dachau concentration camp if they did not move out.

After 1935 the area resembled a large construction site, as over 6,000 tradesmen started to turn the mountainside into a small town, complete with wide range of buildings, roads and security fencing. Building costs soared to 980 million Reichsmarks but nothing would stop Bormann turning Obersalzberg into an impressive complex of buildings. The pinnacle of his building excesses was the Eagle's Nest, a teahouse on top of Kehlstein Mountain.

The Obersalzberg Buildings

The Gutshof

Oberwurf Farm was bought in 1938 and demolished to make way for a large state of the art farm. Bormann's intention was to provide produce for the Berghof and the Barracks, however, the alpine climate was too harsh and the animals produced little. The American Army turned the farm into a recreational centre after the war and it now serves the local golf course.

Villa Bechstein

Helena Bechstein, a member of the famous piano-making family, owned the house next to the Gutshof. She was an ardent Hitler supporter and many Nazi leaders, including Josef Goebbels, used her chalet during visits to Obersalzberg; Mussolini stayed there.

The Wache

The road immediately in front of the Berghof was open to the public during the early days of Hitler's occupation. As his popularity grew so did the crowds hoping to glimpse their Führer, and so did Bormann's concerns for his leader's security. To begin with visitors were asked to respect Hitler's privacy and refrain from shouting or using binoculars but before long the road was cordoned off. A guard tower, built in the style of an alpine gateway, spanned the lower road leading directly to the Berghof and only official visitors were allowed to pass through. Other traffic turned sharp right up the hill towards a second security gate at Platterhof Hotel.

Senior Nazi officials stayed at the Parteigästehaus.

The theatre hall.

Albert Speer's architectural studio.

The SS take over Hotel Zum Türken

Platterhof Hotel

Pension Moritz was the first of many guesthouses on the mountainside. Hitler found Dietrich Eckart living near to the hotel in 1923 and after his release from Landsberg Prison, returned to Obersalzberg. He rented Kampfhäusl, a small chalet situated across the road from the hotel, and often dined in the restaurant. The Nazis bought the hotel from Bruno Büchner in 1936 and remodelled it for party officials visiting Obersalzberg. Two years later the building was torn down and replaced with a modern Volkshotel. Large staff quarters and garages were built nearby. The buildings were converted into convalescent homes for wounded soldiers during 1943.

The buildings were heavily damaged during the air raid in April 1945 but the American Army decided to renovate the ruins and turned them into a US Forces' hotel for troops serving in the area. It was renamed General Walker Hotel, after General Walton Walker, who had served as XX Corps commander in Patton's Third Army. The American Army left in 1995 and five years later the main building was demolished (only the small Skyline Room remains); the visitors' car park covers the area today.

The Parteigästehaus – Party Guest House

Clubheim, a small house just below the Platterhof, was taken over in 1935 and turned into a Guest House for senior Party officials.

The Work Camp

Work started in 1933 and over the next four years *Reichsleiter* Bormann bought and demolished over fifty buildings to make way for the new complex. Work began in earnest in 1937 and hundreds of workers were housed in the Work Camp (*Arbeiterlager*) hidden away in the woods. Bormann's motto 'antreiben, antreiben!', or push on, work faster, was never far from their minds. A large hall capable of housing 2,000 people was built alongside the camp.

Waltenbergerhaus

The Obersalzberg home of Albert Speer, architect of the Nuremberg Rallies and, after 1942, Reich Minister for Armaments and Production, was west of the main work camp. Hitler often spent hours discussing his architectural dreams for a new Germany with Speer. Speer responded by drawing up the Führer's fantastic plans in his studio.

Hotel zum Türken and the SS Barracks (Kasserne)

The need for a permanent guard on the mountain was imperative after Hitler became *Reichchancellor* in 1933. The first step was to take over Hotel zum

Türken. The popular guesthouse and restaurant overlooked the entrance to the Berghof and crowds waited on the terrace, hoping for a glimpse of the Führer. The owner was quickly forced to sell up and the SS guards stationed on Obersalzberg used it as their new barracks. Josef Rasp, Hitler's closest neighbour, living on the slopes in front of the Berghof was also forced to leave.

As Hitler spent more time at the Berghof, Obersalzberg became a centre for Party conferences, military discussions and important diplomatic meetings with heads of state. The SS garrison increased accordingly to maintain security. Three miles of high fencing were built around the Obersalzberg complex, with extra fencing and guardhouses around the Berghof. By the time the Eagle's Nest was finished in 1939, another seven miles had been added on the slopes of Kehlstein Mountain. Locked gates and regular armed patrols kept intruders at bay.

The area immediately behind Hotel zum Türken was levelled as part of Bormann's construction plan and by 1941 four large barrack blocks and a parade ground had been completed. Hotel zum Türken then became the headquarters for the State Security Police. The building was damaged during the bombing in April 1945 but the original owners returned and repaired the damage. The barracks were also badly damaged and the American Army demolished them, turning the area into a soccer field. The area has now been cleared.

Hitler inspects his guards.

The Kindergarten

A school and nursery were added to the rear of Hotel zum Türken to cater for the children of the administrative staff. On warm days the children ran around the playground while the SS garrison paraded a short distance away at the barracks. The building was demolished in 1945.

The Berghof

Hitler wanted his house to be turned into an impressive mountain retreat fit for a country's leader and in 1935 building works started. Architect Alois Degano worked to the Führer's plans, adding large rooms and a new terrace to the existing building. The front of the building was extended and a huge window had pride of place. The frame could be lowered into the basement in warm weather, allowing uninterrupted views of Untersberg Mountain and Salzberg. Staff accommodation was also added with a second driveway for deliveries.

Money was no object and the rooms were filled with expensive furnishings chosen by the Führer, including a six-metre long marble table dominating the meeting room. The building finally reopened in 1936 with a new name – The Berghof.

The Tea House

Conversation filled up large parts of the daily life at the Berghof. A new Tea House was completed at Mooslahnerkopf in 1937 so the Führer could hold relaxed tea parties in private. After lunch Hitler, usually accompanied by his German shepherd dogs, led a procession of friends and visitors down the mountain to the Tea House. The group then gathered in the small building to listen to the Führer's views over drinks and food, often having to endure his endless monologues. Chauffeured cars would always be on standby ready to take the party back up the hillside to the Berghof.

Hitler could relax amongst friends in the Tea House.

Bormann's House

Reichsleiter Martin Bormann chose to occupy Haus Hudler, Dr Seitz's private house overlooking his children's sanatorium. The house was on the western slopes of the highest point on the Obersalzberg where Bormann could watch over the Berghof, keeping a close eye on visitors. It was just one of the many ways that the *Reichsleiter* maintained his iron grip over the close circle of people around the Führer.

The Kindergarten stood alongside the barracks.

Hitler's residence, the Berghof.

The Berghof before the final building work started in 1935.

The Great Hall viewed from the large picture window.

The view of the Untersberg Mountain from the famous window.

Hitler spent hours with Speer, poring over drawings and models.

Hitler preferred the peace and solitude the mountain offered. Albert Speer accompanies him on the path to the Tea House.

Crowds wait patiently in front of the Berghof in the hope of glimpsing the Führer.

Bormann enlarged the building to accommodate his wife and ten children, sparing no expense on the lavish interior decorations and the large outdoor swimming pool. Air raid bunkers were built beneath the slopes behind the house and Bormann had connecting passage-

Bormann's House.

ways to the nearby communications centre and air raid command centre. The bombing raid in April 1945 virtually destroyed the house and the ruins were demolished in 1952. Although parts of the underground system are still intact, they are closed to the public.

Unterwurfl house, on the slope below Bormann's house, was taken over and remodelled for the Obersalzberg's administrative offices. It was bombed in April 1945 and demolished.

Greenhouse (Gewächshaus)

Dr Seitz's sanatorium was knocked down to make way for a large state of the

art greenhouse to grow vegetables and fruit for the complex. As a strict vegetarian, Hitler's plate would be filled with food grown in the greenhouse. The building was built into the side of Adolf Hitler-Höhe, below Bormann's house, and the large retaining wall now forms the perimeter of the hotel car park.

Adolf Hitler-Höhe

The hill behind Bormann's house was renamed Adolf Hitler-Höhe in 1933. A small monument was erected at the summit to commemorate the opening of the first Reichstag under Hitler as Chancellor on 21 March 1933. Ludwig Ganghofer's words 'He whom God

The huge greenhouse catered for Hitler's vegetarian diet.

The memorial commemorating Hitler's appointment as Reichchancellor.

loves, is dropped into Berchtesgadener Land' were inscribed on the monument. It was renamed Göringhügl hill at a later date. A new hotel was recently built, removing large parts of the hill and the eastern part of Obersalzberg has changed forever.

Bormann could watch the Berghof and Hotel zum Türken from his house.

Göring's alpine retreat.

Göring's House

The Nazi Party bought Builcking House, a small mountain lodge on the east side of Göringhügl hill, and gave it to Hermann Göring in 1933. Göring rebuilt the house, doubling its size by 1941, but he still retained many of the traditional alpine features. Again a large outdoor swimming pool was a necessary feature. The chalet's interior décor reflected the *Reichmarschall*'s fascination with outdoor pursuits, in particular hunting. The nearby Hintereck Guest House was demolished to make way for the Adjutant's accommodation and an extensive underground bunker system was built beneath the Göringhügl (rivalries between Bormann and Göring meant that their two systems were kept separate).

Although Göring had left the area before the bombing raid on 25 April 1945, American troops found a large part of his art collection hidden in the tunnels. The raid severely damaged the house and the ruins were removed in 1952. The Adjutant's building is still standing.

Life at the Berghof

After the pressures and formalities of constant public appearances, Hitler was able to relax at the Berghof. From humble beginnings the house grew into a hive of activity with a large staff of housekeepers, cooks and secretaries. Adjutants and orderlies were always close by ready to deal with administration, while chauffeurs were on hand to drive the large fleet of cars. Security was always an issue and the number of SS guards grew from a few dozen to around 2,000. SS-*Obersturmbannführer* Bernhard Frank, one of the members of Himmler's inner circle of twelve SS leaders, led the garrison.

Eva Braun took over from Angela Raubal in 1936 as the informal lady of the house. The simple girl worshipped the Führer and became his constant

Adolf Hitler and Eva Braun enjoy the sunshine on the Berghof's terrace.

companion although she was hidden away during official visits.

Daily life at the Berghof was often monotonous, but no one dared question the Führer's routine. Hitler usually appeared around 11:00 hours and started his day with a long lunch. An invigorating walk down the mountainside to the Tea House usually followed where guests listened politely to Hitler's endless monologues. They were anxious to please and pandered to his tainted views on history, world affairs and politics, fearing a torrent of verbal abuse if they dared to disagree. Films or music followed the evening dinner and then the highlight of the day began as Hitler held court around the fireside, often dominating the conversation as the talk stretched into the early hours.

Hitler had little time for paperwork, unless it was to prepare a forthcoming speech, and his adjutants despaired at the apparent lack of interest in affairs. The Führer preferred to live in a dream world, losing all sense of reality as the years passed and Germany's fortunes declined. Visitors were either left inspired or bewildered after spending time in his company.

As the situation across Europe deteriorated so did Hitler's health and he spent months at the Berghof in 1943 and 1944 to escape the pressures of the war. His physician administered increasing doses of medication but they did not stop the Führer sinking into depression as he became increasingly paranoid.

His suspicions were well founded. On 11 March 1944 General *Feldmarschall* Ernst Busch, Central Army's commander, reported to Obersalzberg. His orderly, Captain Eberhard von Breitenbuch had smuggled a gun into the Berghof and intended to assassinate Hitler. He was made to wait in a side room and never got close to the Führer. Graf von Stauffenberg visited the Berghof twice in July 1944 intending to kill Hitler with explosives. The opportunity never arose and Hitler left Obersalzberg for the last time on 14 July. Six days later Stauffenberg seized his chance in the Wolf's Lair in East Prussia. The Führer was injured in the blast but the expected coup did not materialise and Stauffenberg and hundreds of others suspected of playing a part in the conspiracy were imprisoned or executed.

SS-*Obersturmbannführer* Bernhard Frank kept guard over the Berghof until May 1945 and agreed to evacuate his garrison to prevent Berchtesgaden being razed to the ground by the advancing Americans. His men torched the building before they left and GIs of the 3rd Division found the smouldering ruins deserted.

Diplomatic and Political Centre

A government airport was opened nearby in 1933 for visiting Nazi officials and dignitaries and a fleet of cars was always on hand to take them to the Berchtesgadener Hof Hotel or direct to the Berghof. The flood of visitors, including kings, prime ministers, foreign ministers and ambassadors,

The Duke and Duchess of Windsor pose for the cameras on the steps of the Berghof.

Hitler and Mussolini; the two dictators leave the Berghof together.

Above: British Prime Minister Neville Chamberlain, and Italian dictator Mussolini, visited the Berghof during the Sudetenland crisis.

Left: The front of the Berghof with its huge window.

Below: The Berghof's final appearance.

Hitler welcomes David Lloyd-George, Great Britain's Prime Minister during the Great War, to the Berghof.

increased in 1936 when work on the Berghof had been completed, and it soon became a centre for national diplomacy and political intrigue.

On arrival in Berchtesgaden, either by car or by train, visitors were driven up the steep road to Obersalzberg where an impressive welcome committee would be waiting. The British ex-prime minister, Lloyd-George was extremely impressed by Hitler's courtesy and the surroundings during his visit on 3 September 1936. Although charming on occasions, Hitler sometimes used the Berghof to intimidate statesmen. The visit of Kurt Schuschnigg, the Austrian Chancellor, on 12 February 1938 was a prime example. Hitler waited with three generals, including General Wilhelm Keitel, Chief of the *Wehrmacht* High Command; the message was clear. Hitler humiliated the Austrian Chancellor with outpourings of hatred for the old Austria and after making veiled threats of military action, retired for lunch. After a two-hour wait, Foreign Minister von Ribbentrop presented a document outlining Austria's submission to German political control. In the arguments that followed, the Austrian Chancellor was given an ultimatum; he had three days to submit to Hitler's demands.

Schuschnigg tried in vain to resist but as Nazis rioted across Austria, the Chief of Police invited the German Army across the border to restore order. On 12 March Germany and Austria were united and the *Anschluss* was sealed in an overwhelming vote of approval four weeks later. Although it had been a bloodless coup, Schuschnigg and 76,000 men and women were rounded up by the Gestapo and thrown into concentration camps such as Dachau. Few survived.

As Hitler's expansion plans increased, the predominantly German-speaking border area of Czechoslovakia, the Sudetenland, was his next target. Hitler invited British Prime Minister Neville Chamberlain to attend preliminary discussions at the Berghof in September 1938. Further discussions in Bonn and Munich led to the signing of a Munich Agreement, handing over the Sudetenland to Germany. Chamberlain returned to Britain and announced that he had secured peace for the foreseeable future; he had been seriously misled. German troops marched unopposed into the rest of Czechoslovakia the following March.

The Eagle's Nest

To the south is the Eagle's Nest, a small Tea House on the summit of Kehlstein Mountain. The building was erected so the Führer could hold meetings while admiring the magnificent views over Konigsee Lake and the surrounding mountains. Martin Bormann first mentioned the idea of a road leading to the top of the mountain to Fritz Todt in the autumn of 1936. On 8 November Bormann met the engineer August Michahelles, and in his usual brusque manner he outlined an urgent plan for the road. Michahelles climbed the

Work begins on the mountain-top structure.

Kehlstein the following day and gave Bormann his thoughts on the project and the difficulties it would present. Bormann was determined to push ahead and a month later the NSDAP purchased 900 acres of the mountain from the Bavarian State Forest Administration for 800,000 Reichmarks.

Two engineering companies, Sager and Woerner and Polensky and Zöllner, were instructed to start work in the New Year even though there was deep snow covering the Obersalzberg. Ludwig Grosfl and Hans Weber set about organising the project, building the main road and a service road for construction traffic. Almost at once there were problems and on 1 April a new Chief Engineer, Hans Haupner, was appointed to coordinate the works. Bormann immediately instructed him to reroute the road around along the south side of the mountain and engineers had to survey the precipitous slopes in extreme wintry conditions. He also mentioned the possibility of building a structure at the summit for the first time. Hitler already made daily visits to the Tea House at Mooslahner, on the slopes below the Berghof, and Bormann thought that a new Tea House on the summit would be the perfect gift from the Nazi Party for the Führer's 50th birthday.

The new ideas radically changed the construction plans and also imposed an impossible completion date but the engineers were in no position to argue with Bormann. He met the architect, Professor Roderick Fick at the end of April and gave him one month to submit an acceptable design. Fick presented his ideas on 8 June and he planned to build a single storey structure clad in granite, that blended into the mountain. The main octagonal room would have windows facing in all directions, while a separate room had views of the Scharitzkehl valley and Königsee Lake to the west. The building also had a kitchen area and terraces would allow guests to dine outside in the summer months.

With the preliminary works complete, construction began in earnest and over 3,500 men were recruited, many of them Austrians with mountain experience. They were housed in five camps near the base of the mountain but conditions were rudimentary and the work was arduous. Beer stations were kept fully stocked and payday was usually a raucous time; the authorities also set up a secret brothel to keep the men entertained.

Work continued throughout the summer months and by June the construction roads were complete and an extra one was started at Bormann's insistence. Despite the tight time restraints, he was adamant that the trees, flora and fauna had to be saved and replanted so that the road blended into the hillside.

Work on a cableway to the summit started in June and fifty of the strongest men dug foundations and carried materials up the mountain by hand. The 1,270 metre long cableway was completed on 2 October, after four months' hard work and materials were immediately transported to the summit, a lift of 670 metres, so that work could start on the building.

Bormann kept a close watch on progress, harassing the engineers or personally chasing up suppliers; no one dared to disappoint the Führer's deputy. Important changes were introduced at the end of June when work was suspended on the Platterhof spur. Todt also suggested an innovative way of reducing the amount of disruption near the summit. A short length of tunnel and an elevator inside the mountain would connect the small car park with the Tea House. A few days later Bormann alarmed the engineers by bringing the completion date forward to July 1938. Hitler was becoming increasingly annoyed by the construction work on the mountain and he wanted it finishing as quickly as possible. The work was disturbing his idyllic mountain retreat.

As pressures mounted, Ludwig Grosfl clashed with Bormann and he was soon replaced by Walter Dimroth. On 10 August a landslide swept away part of the lower section of the road and killed five men, but work continued unabated and the rubble was incorporated into the building works.

Short tunnel sections were added during the summer, and after the rock had been stabilised, the workmen drilled and blasted their way through the mountainside. Deep snow during the winter months drove the workforce underground and tar drums filled with burning coal were used to keep tracks open. Work started on the longest tunnel on the road and at the mountain top men began to dig the elevator shaft and the tunnel; at 6.5 metres in diameter, the design included a service tunnel. Three men were buried in an avalanche on 30 January and although they were rescued, morale plummeted as poor

The workforce toiled around the clock in cramped conditions to complete the project on time.

management and changing instructions constantly interrupted work. Despite the difficulties, progress could not be delayed and the men continued to work around the clock in three eight-hour shifts.

The weather was atrocious from the end of March to the middle of May, leaving the men stranded on the mountain and they often slept in temporary huts close to their worksites, living off emergency rations. Despite the difficulties, the lift shaft and tunnel were finished at the beginning of May and work began on installing the mechanical equipment.

Visitors passed through the huge bronze double-doors and walked along the marble lined tunnel, heated by pipes warming the air to stop condensation. After gathering in the domed hall they entered the large brass passenger carriage that whisked them through the bowels of the mountain to the building above.

Work began on the summit as the weather improved, and hundreds of labourers worked around the clock to level an area for the building. Austrian engineer, Hans Haupner, had new camps installed near the top to reduce the number of man hours lost moving up and down the mountain. Tempers were frequently frayed as contractor Hochtief's tradesmen competed for space in the cramped construction site. Fick's design was a concrete structure clad with granite slabs cut individually at Passau and the completed building had the appearance of a solid stone structure.

Work continued at a furious rate, spurred on by Martin Bormann's random visits. The shell of the building was completed in the summer of 1938 and Hitler visited the building for the first time on 16 September as work started on the interior. The decoration of the building was as lavish as the exterior and Professor Heinrich Michaelis spared no expense as he chose wooden panelling, expensive furniture and furnishings. Several windows could be lowered into the ground so the diners could enjoy the magnificent views of the mountains. Meanwhile, Bormann made sure that the site was restored as soon as possible, replanting trees and vegetation while hundreds of birdhouses were set up to encourage wildlife back onto the mountain. The cost had been phenomenal but the Nazi Party picked up the bill for 30 million Reichsmarks (£100m or $160m in modern currency).

Despite the achievement, Hitler only made fourteen official visits to the building (several unofficial visits were also made), the last one on 17 October 1940. The reasons for his lack of interest in the building were many. Hitler had a fear of heights and the thin mountain air affected his breathing; he also believed the elevator was unsafe.

The Eagle's Nest usually remained empty during the war years, but Eva Braun often travelled to the summit to escape from the official business at the Berghof (Hitler also wanted to keep her out of the public eye). There were occasional banquets and after Eva's sister, Gretl, married Himmler's liaison

The Reception Room.

Robert Ley, with his wife and daughter, enjoy the views with Hitler and Bavarian Gauleiter Wagner while Hitler's adjutant, Julius Schaub, stands to one side; Bormann is just around the corner.

officer, SS-*Obersturmbannführer* Hermann Fegelein in June 1944 the wedding party gathered at the Eagle's Nest (Hitler ordered Fegelein's execution at the Berlin Bunker in April 1945).

The End

As bombing attacks increased across Germany, so did the air defences at Obersalzberg as the SS enlarged the anti-aircraft installations and added fog-screening devices to obscure the target. An extensive underground system was built under the mountain with a communications centre, an anti-aircraft control centre and separate systems beneath the leaders' properties. Again no expense was spared and the tunnels and chambers were lavishly decorated and filled with huge stocks of food and drink. As the end drew near Hitler's entourage tried to persuade him to leave Berlin and move to Obersalzberg before the Russians captured the city. Around eighty of his staff left in March and April to prepare for the Führer's homecoming but he decided to stay in his bunker. He committed suicide alongside Eva Braun on 30 April 1945.

On 25 April, 98 American Mustang fighter planes escorted 275 British Lancaster bombers and Mosquito fighter bombers as they dropped over 1,200 tons of bombs on the Obersalzberg complex. The air-raid warning gave most

The window could be lowered into the floor to give views of the mountains.
The Dining Room.

Eva Braun often visited the mountain retreat.

June 3, 1944, Greta Braun's wedding reception, and inset, the happy couple, Greta with her new husband SS-Obersturmbannführer Hermann Fegelein. Hitler ordered the execution by firing squad of his potential 'brother-in-law' for seeking to flee Berlin a few days before the Führer and Eva Braun committed suicide. Greta was at the Berghof expecting their first baby when her husband was shot. Below: the pine wood-panelled Scharitzkehl room.

of the staff time to reach the underground shelters and only thirty-one were killed. The majority of the buildings were severely damaged, and the Berghof itself was hit by at least two bombs; only the Eagle's Nest escaped serious damage.

On 20 April Hermann Göring had left Berlin and escaped the advancing Russian forces to fly to his Obersalzberg home. When it became clear that Hitler was staying in Berlin, Göring telegrammed the Bunker suggesting that he should take over the leadership of the Reich if the Führer was incapacitated. Bormann interpreted the telegram as an act of treason, and, after years of rivalry, finally got his revenge on the *Reichsmarschall*; Göring was stripped of all his offices and excluded from the Nazi Party. SS-*Obersturmbannführer* Bernhard Frank was also ordered to arrest Göring.

He weathered the air raid in his underground bunker and was then escorted to his castle near Mautendorf. In fear of his life from the SS, he gave himself up to the Americans. He was subsequently tried at Nuremberg where he was found guilty of war crimes and committed suicide hours before he was due to hang.

The Americans Arrive

7th Infantry Regiment reached Berchtesgaden around 16:00 hours on 4 May and after arranging the surrender of the town outside the *Rathaus*, Colonel Wallace sent troops up the mountain to investigate Obersalzberg. They found a scene of deserted devastation. The Berghof was a smoking ruin, badly damaged during the air raid and then set ablaze as the SS garrison withdrew. The Stars and Stripes quickly replaced the swastika outside Hitler's residence as the GIs began exploring the cratered landscape. After twelve years the Nazis' occupation of Obersalzberg was over.

General O'Daniel let the 101st paratroopers and the French troops across the River Saalach as soon as the news reached his headquarters. They eventually reached Berchtesgaden at nightfall and set about completing their orders. 7th Infantry Regiment held an official flag-raising ceremony at the Berghof the following day and then handed the area over to 506th Parachute Regiment as visitors poured into the area looking for souvenirs. Guards were eventually posted to stop unscrupulous soldiers removing items but everything of value had already been removed, leaving Hitler's palatial home a wrecked shell.

The Eagle's Nest survived the bombing raid on 25 April 1945 and soldiers of the 506th Parachute Regiment were the first to climb the mountain (the tunnel was blocked by snow), taking anything they could find as souvenirs of their visit. General Maxwell Taylor was furious when he saw the damage and he ordered guards to surround the building. Over the days that followed, a procession of high-ranking officers rode up the mountain in one of Hitler's Mercedes limousines to see the building.

The Berghof received at least two direct hits.

The target description for the attack on Obersalzberg.

Obersalzberg After the War

The American Army of occupation took over Obersalzberg after the war and set about turning the area into a Recreation Centre. Many of the buildings were razed to the ground but the Platterhof Hotel served as a hostel for visiting GIs.

As early as 1951 the Bavarian Government handed the mountain back to the County of Berchtesgaden and before long tourists were visiting the summit. Over the next ten years the building was returned to its former glory as the number of visitors increased steadily. Recent developments on Obersalzberg have been designed to deal with the thousands of people wanting to visit the Eagle's Nest.

The American Army eventually left in September 1995 and major changes have taken place over the past five years as the Bavarian Government improved the facilities for visitors. The largest change was made between 2003 and 2005 when a large hotel was built on Göringhügl (Adolf Hitler-Höhe), radically changing the eastern part of the area.

The fates of the major structures are listed below:

The SS Barracks and the Platterhof Garages suffered heavy damage.

The Berghof

The ruins were demolished on 30 April 1952 (the anniversary of Hitler's death), leaving only the ground floor garages; these were removed in 1995. The area has been used as a refuse site over the years but the twin driveways and the garages' huge retaining wall can still be seen; the crumbling remains of an air raid shelter entrance can be found nearby in the woods.

The Tea House

The ruins lie mouldering in private woods near the Gutshof.

The Platterhof Hotel

The ruins were rebuilt and the building was renamed the General Walker Hotel in honour of General Walton Walker, XX Corps' commander in Patton's Third Army. It was demolished in 2000 (apart from the Skyline Room) and the surrounding area is now the visitors' car park.

The *Parteigästehaus* just below the Platterhof has disappeared; the Documentation Centre now stands on the site.

Platterhof Garage and Staff Quarters

The ruins were demolished at an early stage and in 2003 the area was turned into a parking area for the buses taking visitors to the Eagle's Nest.

The Gutshof

It was a sports lodge and visitors' centre for a golf course used by the US Army, it still is in use by tourists.

SS barracks and Kindergarten

The ruins were removed and the area was turned into a soccer field. A large flat open space below the buses' waiting area marks the spot.

Greenhouse

The structure was destroyed but the retaining wall now forms a backdrop to the car park in front of the new hotel.

Bormann's House and Göring's House

Both have disappeared but Göring's Adjutant's house is still standing.

The Work Camp and the Entertainment Hall to the west of the main complex have disappeared but Speer's studio and house are still standing; both are private property.

Göring's house was reduced to a smoking ruin.

Right: The disgraced Reichsmarschall was taken into the mountains; he was later captured by American troops.

Below: On trial for his life, all his medals and decorations gone.

Below right: With hours to go before meeting the hangman Göring bit into a cyanide capsule.

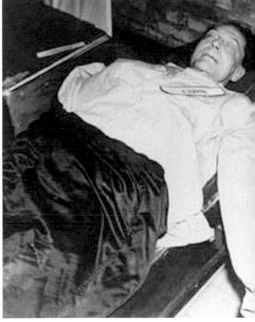

Eagle's Nest

The small building on the summit of Kehlstein mountain escaped damage during the bombing raid and the Bavarian government soon turned it into a tourist attraction. Special buses now take visitors up the steep mountainside to the mouth of the tunnel between May and October (snow permitting).

Hitler's mountain home, reduced to a smouldering ruin, is shortly to become a souvenir hunter's paradise.

Visiting Obersalzberg and the Eagle's Nest

The parking area stands just below the site of the Platterhof Hotel, only the Skyline Room is still standing. Kampfhäusl, Hitler's first home on Obersalzberg, overlooked the car park. The Documentation Centre is just down the slope and the modern building contains a large display charting the rise of the Nazi Party and Hitler's association with the mountain. It is possible to visit part of the tunnels built beneath the mountain and the entrance can be found on the basement floor of the centre. Bare tunnels and chambers give a glimpse of the scale of the underground complex.

Salzburg

The view from the site of the Berghof across Salzburg remains the same. The scene Hitler enjoyed as he planned his conquests.

Hotel zum Turken overlooked the Berghof; Bormann's house was in the trees to the left.

Site of the Bormann's House

Hotel Zum Türken

Berghof Service Road

All that remains of the Berghof is the basement retaining wall.

The Eagle's Nest

Return to the car park and climb the steps leading over to the ticket office for the Eagle's Nest buses. Buses leave at regular intervals but your ticket is only valid for the booked time. If you have plenty of time to spare follow the walk around Obersalzberg but make sure you return to the ticket office in good time. The specially built buses make their way through the woods before beginning the tortuous climb up the side of the mountain. With precipitous cliffs on each side, short tunnels and a tight hairpin bend, the skill of the drivers has to be appreciated. The views across the valleys to the surrounding mountains are spectacular as the bus climbs to the parking area near the top. Before entering the tunnel you must book your return time at the ticket office. Allow one hour unless you intend to dine at the restaurant.

The tunnel leads deep into the heart of the mountain to the lift lobby. The brass lift rises quickly and in a short time the doors open in the Eagle's Nest building. Visitors can wander around the terraces and up the short path to the summit of the

The tunnel leads into the heart of the mountain beneath the Eagle's Nest.

The large brass lift whisked Hitler and his henchmen to the top of the mountain.

The domed waiting room where dignitaries waited for the lift.

The Eagle's Nest today, basks in sunshine.

Huge granite blocks blend the building into the mountain.

mountain. The main part of the building is now a restaurant and the staff request that visitors respect the diners' privacy. Anyone wishing to view the interior of the building can either choose to eat from the reasonably priced menu or join one of the guided tours held at regular intervals. Replica fixtures and fittings have replaced the original furniture removed by looters, returning the building to its former glory.

Directions to the Berghof

There is little left of the rest of the complex and the addition of the new hotel in 2005 has drastically changed the eastern part of the area. It is, however, possible to locate the site of a few of the structures and pinpoint the position of others.

The bus pickup point and the ticket office stand on the site of the Platterhof staff quarters and the garages for the fleet of limousines and other vehicles used by Hitler and his staff. Across from the bus parking area is a large open flat space, the site of the SS barracks. Walk past this area towards the hotel, partially hidden by the trees in the distance. Turn left onto the minor road, noting the large concrete retaining wall (the rear wall of the greenhouses) at the back of the small car park. Continue down the slope under a footbridge. The Kindergarten stood to the left while Martin Bormann's house stood on the slope to the right.

Hotel zum Türken is on the slope to the left, beyond the footbridge. The building was one of the first bought by the Nazis, taken over to stop tourists overlooking the Berghof, and it was used as the SS guardhouse until the new barracks were built. Continue down the hill, past the sentry post, and two overgrown tracks lead off to the left; the driveway and service road to the Berghof. Follow the track into the trees and a huge retaining wall, the rear wall of the garage area beneath the main house. The view across the Untersberg Mountain and Hohensalzburg Fortress on its hill overlooking Salzburg is breathtaking and it is easy to see why Hitler chose the site to escape from the pressures of political and military affairs. The overgrown remains of access shafts are hidden in the nearby woods.

Retrace your route back to your car to complete your tour.

INDEX